RUINED CASTLE

The Search for Jamie Neale and its Aftermath

By Richard Cass

Copyright © 2012 by Richard Cass
All rights reserved.
ISBN: 1-4791-0854-5
ISBN-13: 978-1-4791-0854-1

Cover design © 2012 Richard Cass
Background photo – Mount Solitary – author's photo.
Tarot Cards c/o Builders of the Adytum, 5101 North Figueroa St, Los Angeles, CA90042. http://bota.org
"Permission to use Builders of the Adytum images in no way Constitutes endorsement of the material presented in this work".

Contents

Map of the Jamieson and Cedar Valleys, NSW. i

Chapter One: The Beginning 1

Chapter Two: The Boy 17

Chapter Three: The Journey 29

Chapter Four: The Old Man 39

Chapter Five: The Chopper 55

Chapter Six: The Bush 69

Chapter Seven: The Search 79

Chapter Eight: The Despair 89

Chapter Nine: The Agony 101

Chapter Ten: The Ecstasy 111

Chapter Eleven: The Frenzy 117

Chapter Twelve: The Deal 125

Chapter Thirteen: The Party 133

Chapter Fourteen: The Homecoming 147

Chapter Fifteen: The Betrayal 157

Chapter Sixteen: The Rebuttal 177

Chapter Seventeen: The Consolations of Philosophy 197

Appendices 217

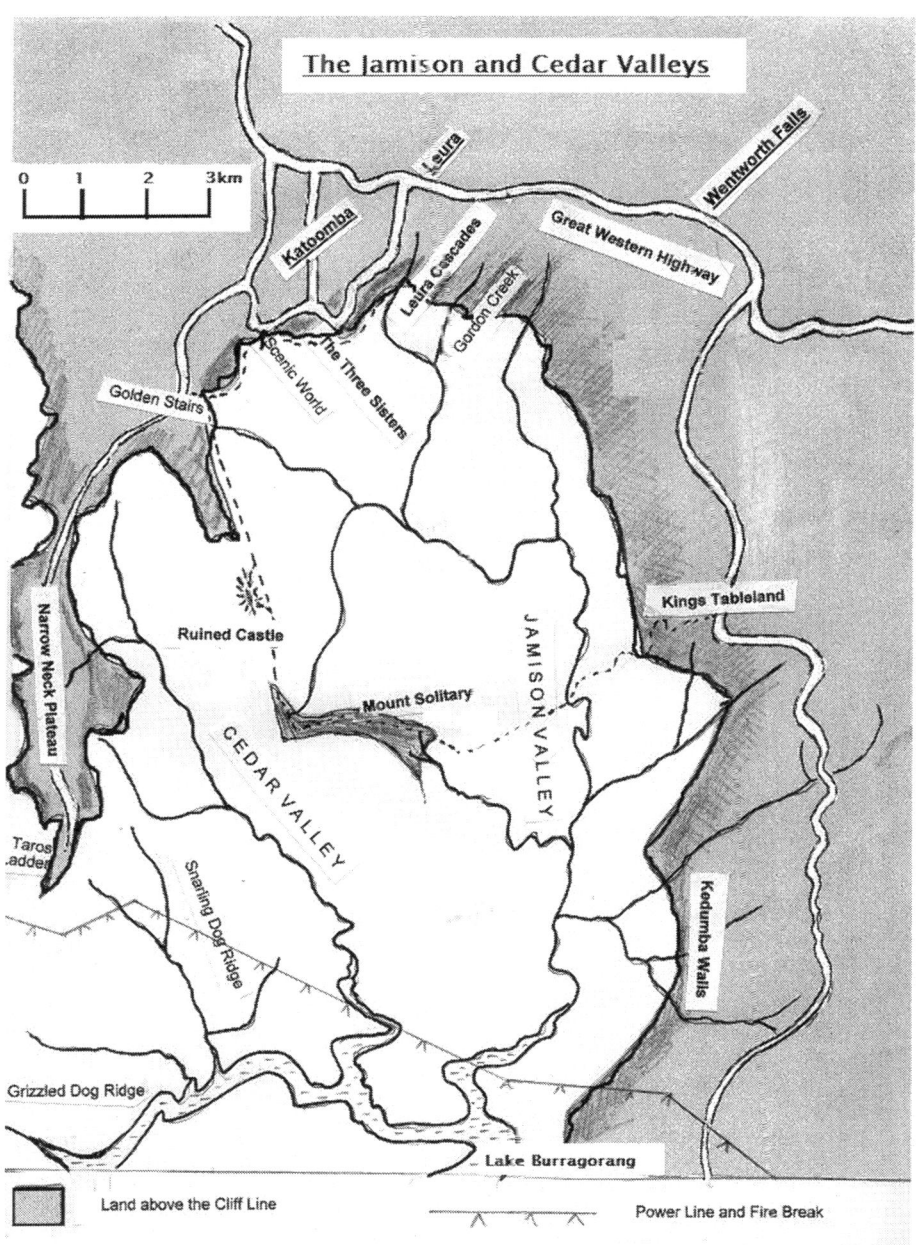

Chapter One

The Beginning

True stories have no beginning. At any rate, they all begin in the same time and place. When the world began. The first man, the first Eden. Eve and the serpent. One thing leading to the next. Until it's things happening today, or a couple of days ago, or the time I leave off fiddling with a copper pipe beneath the floorboards, wipe my hands on a tea towel and go to answer the phone. All because of certain sands that settled on the Triassic sea-bed, or because a man who shared my name left off mending shoes in Yorkshire and washed up in South East Australia. Because that man's great-grandson met, impregnated and married my English mother. The brother my mother bore grew up to invite the son of the second son she bore to visit him in the fine and sunny country he had found, courtesy of poppa's Aussie citizenship, courtesy of that cobbler from Hull.

I picked up the phone. There was a pause then a slight click.

"Hello! This is an important announcement about new government legislation. Do you have debts over £15,000, excluding your mortgage?"

I replaced the phone. After twenty years juggling two jobs and renting out rooms, I was free of debt, excluding the mortgage. Reckoned I was maybe three years away from what Mr Micawber identified as "happiness" - the blissful state of earning more than spending.

Some guy once told me that you either pay for sex or get it for free, 'but ya'll find it's a helluva lot cheaper to pay for it'. In midsummer 2009, I was three years short of settling the tab for the five minutes of fun I got for free in February 1989. In anticipation of the need to support the fallout of that fun through his three years at uni, I had taken on two tenants. It was for their convenience and comfort that I was rerouting the pipe work for the shower. I prefer to take a bath. Previously, the water pipe snaked round the top of the bathroom wall, while power supply followed a white plastic channel round the opposite side. Now both pipe and power cables passed invisibly through the joists above the ceiling. The neatness of the new arrangement would, in due time, justify the expense, blood, sweat, broken fingernails and disruption that had been the story of my week so far. The job was taking longer than I had anticipated. The tenants had already moved in and I was obliged to apologise for prising up the floorboards of their rooms while they were out at work.

As I packed away tools, swept up the mess and laid back the boards, the lad whose prospective uni expenses had prompted this all but finished workmanship was on the other side of the world. Jamie left school the previous summer then returned as a science assistant, covering for someone's maternity leave, saving wages for the trip he was planning in this, his 'gap year' - Australia, Cambodia, Vietnam, Kathmandu. Then off to Moscow. It was a bizarre itinerary. On Monday, 6th July, I had nearly finished sorting out the shower. The boy had been in Australia for a fortnight. Back on the 20th of June, I'd seen him off. We shared an awkward hug. Jamie was a decent kid, but we had not been getting on. Like any modern nineteen year old, he could be truculent. To my mind, he took a mischievous delight in provoking trouble between Jean and me. Said it was my imagination. Recently I had put a shot across his bow, "Don't take the house for granted, I could always leave it to the NSPCC!"

I had intended to present him with some cash in case he got in trouble overseas, but I had worked all night. I was tired and I forgot. By the time I'd gone home and had some sleep I felt better, but he was gone by then. I felt guilty about the way we'd parted. He would be away for three months. I should have done better. I still had the money - about a hundred pounds in US and Aussie dollars. On the following Monday, I posted the money to him, addressed via my brother, with whom he would be staying. Jeff lives in Perth, Western Australia. The letter read as follows:

Dear Jamie,

I enclose funds for use in extremis. Save it for the trip to Indo-China.

I understand that you will not be spending much time at home before rushing off to Exeter. (Feel free to let me know if I've got this wrong!) I am therefore advising you about the financial arrangements I am making for your time at uni.

I will be sending you £5,000 per annum, in three installments. You will get £1,667 in October and similar amounts in January and April. All by cheque. This gives you something like £530 a month for nine months of the year. I anticipate that you will find some other means of support during the summer break. This will definitely not suffice for your needs.

You will probably get something from my mum - make sure you write to thank her if you do. You may also find work at weekends and holidays. Ask local security firms about night work. You will also have access to the student loan system. Good luck.

I look forward to seeing you, however briefly, on your return to civilisation.

— Regards, from your affectionate father.

By the time this letter arrived at Jeff's place, Jamie had moved on. Having spent a week getting to know his three Aussie cousins, he took a plane across to the east coast. By the time he did get to read my letter he was undergoing treatment for malnourishment and exposure and his dad was sitting alongside him. Within a week of that emotional reunion, 'sources' were briefing the world about our 'dysfunctional relationship'.

Jamie did manage to phone me soon after his arrival in Perth. It was a good conversation. We seemed to be getting on a bit better. "I won't be able to see Ho Chi Minh. Not in Hanoi, anyhow. They've sent him back to Moscow for a makeover. Maybe I'll catch up with him when I go to see Lenin".

He asked me why I hadn't done what Jeff had done - emigrated to Oz with Jamie's mum and the rest of the family, taking advantage of the old man's Aussie citizenship.

"It's a great place. Lots of blondes and really cool looking Chinese chicks..."

"Because it's too bloody hot out there!"

After she gave birth to brother Jeff in '52, my mother had sailed off to Melbourne with new husband and baby boy.

Life in the lucky country was not to her liking - an experience aggravated by grinding poverty and her husband's irascible temperament. He commenced blazing rows with the family he had left at fifteen, drank too much and too often and attempted to do away with himself - spent time in a mental health ward. My future teenage mother coped as best she could with a two year old child, a home lacking gas, electricity and running water, a crazy, psychotically jealous husband, in-laws who wanted nothing to do with her and the discovery that she was about to drop another baby; all far from her own friends and relations back in the East End of London. On top of all this, she was constitutionally averse to hot weather and phobicly terrified of snakes in a country that was jumping with them.

In January 1955, Andrew Richard Cass popped out. I was born in the morning traffic jam - Collins Street in the centre of Melbourne. My birth certificate describes place of birth as 'between UR lot 1, Barnett Grove, Noble Park and the Royal Women's Hospital'.

I understand that the hospital is now no longer 'Royal'. The battering I took when I emerged from the bush to bounce bewildered across the hard, grey pavements of mid-century Melbourne was to prove an eerie foretaste of my return to Oz, fifty four years later. I even got a mention in the local paper - one of three babies delivered by the same ambulance driver during the same week. Lousy driver, great obstetrician. I don't know if the guy got paid for the story. If he did, he didn't cut me in.

That summer of 1954/55 was scorchingly hot in south-east Australia. Rose spent most of it sponging and fanning her listless baby boy. Back in the fifties, Australia was a land of opportunity. A land that rewarded hard graft and offered every white bloke his chance to get on, with the proviso that you were expected to stand on your own two feet and pay your own way. Mum came from a different land - a land that no longer exists. She was raised in post-war West Ham in the East End of London. Back in the late forties, this was a close-knit and neighbourly place, where people helped out. They shared the good times - particularly when those good times involved the receipt of stolen goods - and rallied round when you were down on your luck. This was the East End that, only a few years before, had endured the Blitz. Rose was evacuated to Norfolk while bombs were falling. Grey, post-war years of rationing and austerity encouraged a network of neighbourly relationships aimed at circumventing regulations, through theft, fraud and spivs, to ensure that no Cockney went short. The work ethic was strictly rationed.

As she wiped sweat from my face beneath that relentless fair weather of Australia, rats gnawing at the rusks that fell from my pushchair, Rose missed friends and family, dreamt of pea-souper fogs and frosty ferns on window panes. The last straw came when some kids found a snake to drag round the trailer park.

One year later, the four of us - Rose, husband John, my brother and me - arrived in England on the SS Uganda. Waiting on the dockside at Tilbury were my English Nan and English Aunts. I was destined never to meet any relations on my father's side. There was ice crinkling underpram and, for the first time in my life, I could see what my own breath looked like. Though fifth generation Australian born, I was to be raised an Englishman. Just like mum, I adored chilly weather. I could never tolerate the midsummer heat in the land of my birth. When my own son was born, he too grew up to love the cold and sweat like a scrunched sponge in the summer. Grandma's genes. Genes that would save his life.

I was grateful for Jamie's phone call. Within a fortnight I was to become convinced that it had been the final conversation with the son who had delighted and exasperated me for the previous nineteen years. For the moment, it just felt good that he had taken the trouble to phone. We were getting on a bit better now. I felt appreciated. Jamie was a son I could be proud of.

When I sent off the letter about arrangements for Jamie's time at

Exeter University, I included a covering letter for his host, my brother Jeff. Jeff had been born in London soon after our parents married. He had been named John, after his father, but became 'Jeff' through *soi-disant* but misspelt identification with World Cup hero Geoff Hurst. In 1985, Jeff had taken his family to live in Perth, Western Australia. At that time he had a wife and two daughters. In WA he gained another daughter and a divorce. By the time Jamie came to stay, Jeff was living with a new partner, Maureen.

The letter I sent to Jeff now seems pretty prescient. I may have failed to identify the place where he would duly screw up but I certainly spotted the 'dangerous deficiency of self-doubt', the Hubris that so nearly led to Nemesis and a lonely grave beneath fallen eucalyptus leaves.

22nd June 2009

Dear Jeff,

I trust that the boy arrived without mishap in the land that gave the world Rolf Harris. I was a bit tired and testy when we made our farewells as I had worked overnight. I had meant to slip him a few bob to dip into in the event of emergency. I forgot to do it - so I enclose the cash in the attached envelope. I would wish him to hang on to this money for use in extremis, e.g. a taxi fare to the British Embassy, after he's been fleeced and beaten shitless somewhere on the road to Mandalay. He reckons Indo-China is a safe part of the world. I recall that this is the same holy fool who blundered into a spot of bother with local low-life within minutes of stepping off a train in Colwyn Bay. He had confused Colwyn with Conwy, where we were waiting for him. If he happily returns to Blighty, his progress unsullied and funds unbroached, he can take the money to Exeter with him in October. He'll certainly need it there.

I haven't a clue what he's intending to do in your neck of the bush. He may deign to enlighten you. He may keep his cards close to his chest or he may not have much of a clue himself.

Don't worry about him and don't feel you have to put yourself out for him. He's pretty gauche, very naïve and dangerously deficient in self-doubt. I suppose we were much the same ourselves at nineteen. He assumes what people are saying, rather than listens to what they say. He tends to finish other peoples' sentences for them, invariably getting it wrong. He takes a peculiar interest in things which others may find odd - like the cadavers of communist dictators. He could certainly have turned out worse and I'm lucky to have him, but he's not, by any chalk, a younger version of me. Deo Gratias. Many thanks for taking him in.

You will be aware of plans that are also afoot to fly Clair over to Oz sometime in September, along with our lady mother. I suspect that each of them nurtures a rosy notion of how easy it will be to get on with the other.

I confidently predict that they will be hardly on speaking terms by the time they get back to Britain. I wish you all the best in managing all three arrivals.

I am likely to be getting a lot less teaching work next term, due to the less balmy financial climate - unless swine flu rampages through the pedagogic population like some scourge of God. In anticipation of this financial pinch, I've recently taken on two new tenants. One's a Dutchman, disconcertedly reminiscent of a younger Sven Goran Eriksson. The other is just a bit of a lad. He's been doing up the room prior to moving in in July, but I'm already finding him an irritation. I've been tenant-free since you were over here in October. Now that Jamie's off to uni and the teaching's dried up, I need the dosh. So I'll just have to put up with the sundry inconveniences of communal living until he graduates. Roll on 2012!

Regards from,
— Your affectionate brother, Rick.

I had spoken to Jamie's mother sometime in the previous weekend. She was a bit surprised that she hadn't heard anything from Jamie for a few days but she wasn't worried. He must be enjoying himself too much to find the time to phone. It was South-East Asia that we were worried about. Only one month before, Princess Eugenie had been robbed in Phnom Penh, despite being escorted by Royal Protection Officers. They had been unable to hang on to her assailant due to the hostility of the crowd. Jamie would be on his own and temperamentally inclined to argue rather than let it go.

After slamming down the phone on that 'important announcement about new government legislation', I got back to work, nailing down floorboards and rolling back displaced carpets. The phone rang again. They just never give up! For a second or two, my mood lightened. Instead of the anticipated spiel about debt management, I recognised Jeff's voice. He had picked up an Aussie accent from his quarter century in Perth.

"Rick, have you heard about Jamie? He's gone missing!"

The pleasure evaporated. "What do you mean?"

"He was staying in a place called Katoomba. It's a holiday resort in the Blue Mountains. The police have called me and say they're worried about him".

Jeff explained that the New South Wales Police had contacted him because his name and number were on the mobile phone that Jamie left behind at the Katoomba Youth Hostel. He had last been seen leaving the hostel on the previous Friday morning. In New South Wales it was now Monday night.

"You need to speak to a guy called Dallas Atkinson. He's handling the investigation, but you won't get him till the morning. They're ten hours ahead of you".

I was numb with dread; 'police' and 'missing' are words to strike fear into any parent. Had he been kidnapped? Murdered? Or both? I tried to phone Jamie's mother, Jean, but got no reply. I wasn't even sure she needed to know. Perhaps it was better to wait till I knew what had happened to our baby.

I thought she might be out with her adult son Gary, the child of an earlier marriage. I realised that my mobile phone was in my car and, when I retrieved it, I saw that there had been many messages and missed calls. On the voicemail there was a message from Dallas Atkinson, asking me to contact him urgently. Gary had rung too. I phoned him. He was out shopping with his mother. They knew that Jamie had gone missing. Jean was okay. She was handling it better than I had expected. At this time I had not yet read Peter Pierce's fine exploration of 'an Australian anxiety' - entitled *'The Country of Lost Children'*. It was a book I read as background to writing this one. *'The Country of Lost Children'* opens with various accounts of children lost in the bush in the nineteenth century. Some survive their ordeal. Some don't. The second part of the book investigates the disappearance and destruction of children in more recent times, through darker forces - neglect, exploitation and foul play. The book quotes a long passage from a short story by Henry Lawson. Pierce introduces this passage as an 'arresting vignette of the search component of the lost child narrative'.

> "*I could see it all. She and the half-caste rushing toward where the children were seen last, with Old Peter after them. The hurried search in the nearer scrub. The mother calling all the time for Maggie and Wally, and growing wilder as the minutes flew past. Old Peter's ride to the musterers' camp…The hurried search the first day, and the mother mad with anxiety as the night came on. Her long hopeless, wild-eyed watch through the night, starting up at the sound of a hoof and reading the worst in one glance at the rider's face. The systematic work of the search-parties next day and the days following…"*

(Henry Lawson, '*Joe Wilson and his Mates*', Edinburgh: Blackwood, 1901)

When I heard that my 'child' was missing, his mother and I were twelve thousand miles away from where the lad had last been seen. We could not even get hold of the officer in charge of the investigation, let alone analyse his glance. It was a sunny afternoon in England, but we were helpless. There was nothing we could do to deal with this sudden and shocking information. We could only talk to each other and wonder what was happening to Jamie as we talked. I googled 'Katoomba'. The town was about seventy miles west of Sydney. The map showed plenty of paths and roads around the place. It was not possible to walk twenty miles in a straight line without crossing a road. How was it possible for a fit young man to get lost and not find a road? Jamie could have walked nearly a hundred miles in the four days he had been missing.

I remembered my own misadventures at the age of nineteen. In 1974, I had travelled to Ireland in its time of troubles. I had been looking forward to seeing the remote and romantic coast of County Mayo. Soon after I got there, I was indecently assaulted by the Youth Hostel warden who placed his hand over my groin as I lay half asleep.

"Can I tie a knot in it for you?"

There were plenty of men out there for whom teenage youths were achingly desirable. My own unpleasant encounter brought no serious consequences. Like most young men, I was destined to shrug off plenty more of these proposals before my loss of the bloom of youth curtailed such overtures. Others had not been so lucky. I had once lived in the same street as Denis Nilsen, a serial killer of feckless young men. Perhaps my son had had the misfortune to meet another Nilsen.

Or maybe he had been murdered for his PIN number. Over the years, there had been distressing cases of travellers forced to divulge these details by killers who go on to drain their victim's bank account. It did not bear thinking about. I googled 'Blue Mountains', together with 'missing'. The results chilled me to the bone; so many missing tourists. Why wasn't this front page news? In 'Jaws' - Spielberg's flick about a resort haemorrhaging teenagers to the eponymous great white shark - there is a sub-plot whereby the mayor publicly pooh-poohs the problem, determined to safeguard his town's status as a tourist attraction. What was happening in the Blue Mountains?

In January two French tourists had disappeared, aged 21 and 22. Only one month ago, a local barman had vanished on his way home from work. A killer on the loose? Who was covering all this up?

The tragic case of David Iredale also featured strongly in the results. David died of dehydration in the Australian summer of 2007. He had been bushwalking in order to gain his Duke of Edinburgh Award. Jamie himself had orienteered through Epping Forest in that same year with the same end in view. I did not yet know that the Iredale tragedy occurred on the same route that Jamie had taken. It was only after I arrived in Katoomba and spoke to the police that I learnt that the lost Frogs turned up safe and sound and the missing local bloke had had 'issues'. Issues-bloke had gone missing of his own volition and actually resurfaced while the search for Jamie was at its height.

As I sat glued to my computer on that dreadful afternoon, I became increasingly worried that some terrible crime was behind his disappearance, all the while still hoping that he had simply got lost and was wandering round in circles. It was incredibly frustrating to be so helpless when a loved one was in trouble, but there was nothing I could do but wait for more news and hope it was good news. I knew he was missing but did not know why. I wanted to do something to help find him but, for now, there was nothing I could do, except google, and what came up on Google did very little to reassure me.

I took Jeff's call at about twelve noon. At twenty five minutes past two, my mobile phone bleeped. It was a message from 'Jamie'. I grabbed the phone and quickly flicked through the menus to bring up the text.

The message read; *'Prince henry cliff 2nd path 2nd lookout'* (sic.).

It was not the kind of message I expected from a son who had been reported missing for four days. Why not *"I'm OK!"* or *"I'm lost"* or *"Help!"* The mention of a cliff seemed pretty ominous, though not for one moment did I think Jamie was suicidal. Hadn't Jeff just told me that the police had Jamie's phone? Who had sent me this bizarre text?

I rang Jamie's phone, which transferred me to the answering service. I left a message asking him to call. I said we were worried about him. Call me or your mother. I couldn't understand why he couldn't take the call. The text had been sent only seconds before. Maybe he was in a region of poor reception. I texted a message to the phone. *"Whoever has this phone please contact me"*. I phoned again, left a message for 'whoever has got this phone'. Nothing seemed to get a response.

Was he stranded on the Prince Henry Cliff Path? My dread was that somebody had just dumped his remains there and had sent the message, either in mockery or through conscience, to let his dad know where the body could be found. I googled 'Prince Henry Cliff Path'. There was such a path in Katoomba. This made it seem likely that the message had some kind of relevance to what was happening, but what on earth did it mean?

Another source of anxiety was the e-mail received by Jamie's sister, Clair. It had been sent on the Thursday - one day before Jamie's disappearance. Clair felt it was unlike him to send an e-mail without either text or defined 'subject'. Nor did she recognise the Hotmail e-mail address that he had used to send it. Jamie normally took the trouble to compose a suitably sardonic one-liner to serve as 'subject' There were photos attached to this textless e-mail message, pictures of Australian wildlife - kangaroo, koala, kookaburra. No pictures of Jamie. Or anyone else for that matter. It was as if someone were playing games with us, someone anxious to give the impression Jamie was alive but someone who didn't really know how he went about things. It was only after Jamie emerged from the bush that he was able to explain that he had e-mailed the pictures in a hurry. He had bought his internet time by the hour and thought he was about to lose the connection when he sent this 'message'.

At the time it just seemed very odd.

For the moment, all we could do was worry and wait. I was alone in Watford, Jean with her family in Muswell Hill. I sat in front of my computer, transfixed by that litany of English tourists for whom the lucky country had proved anything but. Peter Falconio, from Huddersfield - flagged down by a man with a dog and never seen again. His girlfriend managed to struggle free after being bound and gagged by his assailant. Brian Hagland from North London - punched to death while walking on Bondi Beach. Police say he may be the victim of, quote, 'a wave of motiveless, thrill-seeking killings that are sweeping the area'. Thanks, guys. Seven backpackers butchered by a guy called Ivan Millar in the nineties - rumours that he had accomplices who were never caught. There is no shortage of violent, crazy people running amok in North London. Indeed Jamie had himself been robbed at knifepoint as he walked home from school at fifteen. I certainly had worries about his safety in South-East Asia but I anticipated no problem with his time in Oz. The language was mostly mutually intelligible with his own English, the police efficient and incorruptible and the general population tolerant and laid back.

When I wasn't scaring myself silly, I just lay on the bed, staring at the ceiling. The sultry summer afternoon darkened to evening and the night.

As soon as it was eight o'clock in Australia, eleven o'clock at night British Summer Time, I called the number that Jeff had given me for Dallas Atkinson. I was told Dallas was at Blackheath, another Police Station. I phoned the new number and got through to Dallas. I quickly asked him about whether the police had the phone. I told him about the message. He explained that the text had been present as a draft message on Jamie's phone. It had been forwarded to me in error while the police examined the phone in hopes of extracting any information about Jamie's movements, acquaintances or intentions. It would have been nice if they could have let me know at the time they sent it, instead of putting me and Jean through nearly nine hours of anguish.

Dallas said they had a good idea of Jamie's movements up to the Friday morning when he had set off on a bushwalk. He had spent one night in a hostel in King's Cross, a run-down part of Sydney. He had visited a wildlife park in Sydney, where he had his photo taken with a koala bear. He had made his way to Katoomba on Thursday, checked into the YHA and expressed interest in a bushwalk. He had been up early on Friday to watch the sun rise as it lit up the local scenery, returned to the hostel for an hour, then set off on his walk. He had booked to go on a tour of some local caves on the Saturday, but failed to show up. I spoke about my fears that someone was laying a false trail, through the strange e-mail that Clair had received. Dallas asked me to forward the e-mail message to him. He, in turn, would send me the picture that had been left behind in Katoomba YHA. Could I confirm that this was my son? When the picture arrived, my doubts were allayed. It was my Jamie posing alongside an enormous, sleepy-eyed koala. I told Dallas that I would be flying out to the Blue Mountains as soon as I could get a flight. I saw myself driving around the back roads of the search area, calling out his name above the cliffs, till sometime I encounter a shambling, emaciated figure stumbling along some dirt road to nowhere. Jamie cannot believe that it is his dad who has found him. We embrace, overcome with relief that all will be well and I carry his broken body, scourged by the bush, back to the van. I could not sit frustrated at home, while others were searching for my son. I was going to fly over to Australia and find him myself.

Chapter Two

The Boy

I am not a great fan of soap opera, but I did get into 'Soap' in the late seventies. This was an American sitcom, ostensibly in the form of a soap, which followed the bizarre escapades and tangled relationships of two families, the families of two grown up sisters - Jessica Tate and Mary Campbell. The plot lines were so routinely 'over the top' that you sometimes wondered whether the soap opera format could survive the relentless parody. One plot line exploited the mayhem that came about through the arrival of 'Alien Burt'. This extraterrestrial was able to simulate the appearance of Mary's husband, Burt, in order to consummate a passion for her. The situation precipitated a predictable comedy of errors. At one point a distraught Burt pleads for his wife not to take notice of anything the alien has to say. "Listen to me, please listen to me. Whatever you do.... don't listen to me!"

Later on, Mary herself became aware of the masquerade but, by then, the damage has been done. Having fallen pregnant at about this time, her first question at the baby's birth was "What colour is it? White? ... Or Silver?"

When Jamie joined the great soap opera of life back in November 1989, I was there to see it happen. I had intended to leave when the strain got tough, but, figuratively speaking, Jean took it all in her stride. Before

I knew what was going on, a silver and purple mass of toes and testicles tumbled out into the world.

"It's a boy!" I said, tentatively.

It was not quite what I had been expecting. His sister had arrived the previous year. Clair had been a beautiful baby with big, vulnerable blue eyes and translucent, pale, almond blossom skin. This one was by no means a beautiful baby. By the time the hospital staff had swabbed away the silvery grey scum that had given him his metallic sheen and the blood in his extremities had calmed down after the exertion of worming through Jean's pelvis, he looked marginally better.

"Aha... Looks almost human!" I quipped, relieved that Jean had not, after all, had sex with extra-terrestrials behind my back. I was not to be allowed to forget this remark.

Four years later, I took the children on holiday to Heacham on the west coast of Norfolk. The previous year I had also taken the children away on holiday, but I had done so by kicking down their mother's door, scooping them into my arms and driving off with them to Swanage. Holidays with the children were important to me. I worked long hours and, by the spring of that year, I was no longer living with Jean. Holidays were a rare chance to be with my children when they woke up and when they went to bed. I enjoyed sharing their excitement about the prospect of going away, enjoyed watching chubby toddler legs race across a sandy beach or paddle in a rock pool. When Jean cancelled the holiday for 1992, she hit me where it hurt and she bloody well knew it.

Two days after I kidnapped them, I phoned Jean to let them know they were okay. After I'd brought them back, she took out an injunction forbidding me from approaching the house. It was done 'ex-parte', which means that the bloke finds out about it when he gets the injunction through the post. What about my side of the story? My 'parte'? As a matter of fact, I had already made an application in a neighbouring court for a contact order. I was amazed that the court was prepared to listen to one side while the excluded party was so obviously anxious to settle things in a peaceful manner. What made the ruling even more galling was that the injunction form had the prefix 'DV' - domestic violence. I have never struck Jean or the children. Jean's grounds for excluding me from the lives of the children were based upon the assertion that 'the respondent is an Australian'. She said I was likely to take the children over to Australia. It took me nine long months to get the court to listen to me. I did get to meet my children a few times during this period, but only under conditions of stifling and humiliating supervision. One such encounter was a 'contact meeting' in the presence of a Court Welfare Officer. Jean had been required to bring the children to the meeting so the Welfare Officer could ascertain the children's feelings about contact with their father. This lady would then prepare a report which would provide a non-partisan overview of matters in contention. At one point Jean was asked to leave the room in order that the Welfare Lady could gauge whether the children became distressed at finding themselves left behind with their father. Clair and Jamie made no effort to follow their mother. They simply carried on chatting and playing with me. At one point, Jamie toddled up to me with arms outstretched for a hug. It was brilliant. He was not yet able to talk, but he was making his feelings clear. The report was positive. I got all the access I asked for, along with two weeks holiday a year with the children. It had been a chastening experience. This happened before 'Fathers for Justice' and their caped crusader capers. Despite being advised that judges are 'invariably courteous and helpful' to unrepresented litigants, I met with judicial rudeness that still causes my blood to seethe at the remembrance of it. My beloved children were put through a separation little short of bereavement on the basis that their father spent a year in Australia as a baby. It's enough to make any man dress as Batman.

The holiday in Heacham was the first chance to take advantage of that final settlement. Some of my fondest memories of that sunshiny August week in West Norfolk involve our trip to the ruins of Castle Rising. This is a fairly compact Norman keep, surrounded by a grassy concentric mound. The children were too young to be told that this was where Isabella, the 'She-Wolf of France', had been imprisoned by her son, Edward III. Edward was the most illustrious of England's Plantagenet kings. He had come of age in 1330 and seized the reins of power from Isabella and her paramour. Three years earlier, Isabella had arranged for the boy's pathetic father, Edward II, to be spit roasted per anum in mockery of his homosexuality. It was not a tale to share with a five year old child, but Clair and Jamie relished their day at the castle.

In the fourteen years that followed this holiday, there would be plenty more encounters with relics of the nation's bloody past and, as the children matured in their understanding, Jamie, more so than Clair, proved receptive to the allure of history. Together, we scrambled over castles at Manorbier, Harlech, Dunstanburgh, Oystermouth, Cilgerran and Pembroke, along with abbeys at Cleve, Whitby and Rievaulx. By the time he reached his teens, it was Jamie who insisted we visit the Tudor bastion of St Mawes, beside the River Fal. On our last holiday as a family, when Jamie had reached the age of seventeen, he took off to explore Conwy Castle and the medieval town walls by himself. I had passed on the flame. This was the same week that Jamie, Clair and I set out for the summit of Mount Snowden. As I trudged painfully round the horseshoe ridge that leads to the peak, Jamie appeared behind me. He was supposed to be well ahead of me, but had missed the path. This is, of course one of the most well-trodden paths in the country, negotiated by millions of other walkers without difficulty. That boy could get lost on a croquet lawn.

When the time came for Jamie to choose subjects to study at 'A' level, he opted for history, among others. I was pleased that he found the subject worthy of his study, but disappointed that the syllabus concentrated on the recent past, (including my own lifetime!), rather than medieval times. One Sunday afternoon I asked him whether he knew where Karl Marx was buried. He reckoned Marx was probably mouldering on the continent somewhere - maybe Germany or Russia.

"Let's go and see him," I said. "He's a couple of miles down the road".

We arrived at Highgate Cemetery just as they were shutting up, slipped through the spiked iron gates while keepers were ushering everyone else out. We soon located the massive stone bust of the revolutionary old fool and chatted for a while to a thirty-something Polish bloke who was there to pay his respects. Not every Pole was pleased to see the walls come tumbling down, it seemed.

Now that my son was old enough to choose his own recreation, we spent less time in each other's company. It felt good to share this adventure in search of a dead philosopher. The prescribed weekend contact visits were played out by this time, but things had got much better between Jean and me. She was happy to see me and she had come along to most of the holidays that I had wrung from her in County Court.

Jamie seemed to get a buzz out of his close encounter with the ghost of Marx. He was not a communist sympathiser but academic immersion in the history of the twentieth century left him acutely aware of the shadow cast by Karl Marx. Millions of men and women had lost lives and freedom at the behest of regimes which purported to revere this man's political and economic analysis. Yet here he slept this peaceful plot in an up-market suburb of London, heedless of squirrels and song-birds that rustled round his resting place. 'Workers of the World Unite,' proclaimed the words beneath his portrait bust. Like the bluster of Shelley's *'Ozymandias'*, it was a monument to the futility of political fashion.

It was a pleasant excursion - a throwback to the days when I could carry Jamie on my shoulders as we explored the past together. I did not, at the time, realise how deeply Jamie had been affected by the encounter until, two years later, I saw his gap year travel itinerary. I was astonished - and perturbed - to see that he was flying to Vietnam and Moscow, as well as visiting Uncle Jeff in Australia. Having called on the corpse of Karl Marx, he said he wanted to drop by on Ho Chi Minh and Lenin too. In spite of my worries, I recognised that it was a unique and brilliant conceit to tour the world by way of close encounters with the cadavers of communist dictators. I would have preferred to watch it all on TV, presented by Michael Palin or Michael Wood perhaps, with a camera crew on hand in case things went wrong.

Long before this wonderful boy was born, when I was a teenager myself, I had read about the total eclipse of the sun due to take place over Cornwall in 1999. It was in my mother's 'Prediction' magazine. The eclipse was to be a sign that the great war with China was nearing its climax, but Britain would survive the crisis. Thirty years later, with no oriental war band on the horizon, Jamie and I headed west to join the fun. Maybe we could sacrificially slaughter an Exmore pony or two to the great god, Helios, just to make sure the world didn't end when the sun went dark. Jamie was nine years old. We had to sleep in the back of a Morris Maestro van. Clair had to be content with viewing the partial eclipse from North London. This was to be a father and son bonding road trip. I stopped for a Polish hitchhiker on London's North Circular Road. Amazingly, he too was off to Cornwall to experience 'totality'. We discussed Grimms' Law as we headed down the M4 - pyre and fire, pipe and fife, vulpa and wolf. Latin 'p' becomes Germanic 'f'. The rain lashed down as we drove across Dartmoor in the night, frogs by the million hopping over the road. At four in the morning, we parted company in the Cornish town of Liskeard, Tomas still bearing westward. I turned south - headed for Looe, searching for a place to park up and sleep.

For the next three days we slept in the van, peed in public toilets and fried eggs on the beach. In the event, the eclipse was a disappointment - sun obscured behind clouds at this moment I'd waited thirty years to see. As those ten seconds of darkness engulfed us, my son and I sat it out on a cliff overlooking the sea between Seaton and Looe. Life was good.

The best time we had on this adventure had actually been the night before - Quiz Night at The Downderry Inn. We wrote our team's name down as 'The Muswell Hillbillies', but my 's' was misread. It was 'The Mugwell Hillbillies' who came second in the quiz, despite a plethora of locally biased questions. How the hell was I expected to know Plymouth Argyle's latest shirt sponsor?

Along with the cuddle I got from Jamie at the Court Welfare Officer's interview, this was one of those moments to savour down the long years of fatherhood. We went on to enter a few more quizzes when Jamie reached his late teens. We still called ourselves 'The Mugwell Hillbillies', though we seldom lived up to our early promise. On one such occasion, I suggested a change of name. "How's about 'The Numbskull Wears Prada'?"

It was a decent enough play on words, but the boy in the *Prada* t-shirt was not a numbskull and resented the cruelty of the jest. It lacked the element of truth so essential to hyperbolic humour. We stuck with 'The Mugwell Hillbillies'. The *Prada* t-shirt went on to forge a career on Australia's Channel Nine.

In Classical Greece, supreme happiness for a man was encapsulated by the career of Diagoras of Rhodes. Diagoras won the boxing contest at the Olympics and then, twenty-four years later, watched his son win the same competition. As his sons led him round the stadium in triumph, Diagoras died of happiness. There is a great deal of satisfaction to be had in seeing one's child develop year by year into something similar to oneself. Whether through genes or parental guidance, Jamie came to share my interest in history and philosophy. He was likeable and articulate, but prone to resent an insult and tenacious in denying his own shortcomings. Though I came to love and admire my son, he complained that I failed to give him credit for his achievements. I had a habit of countering any element of knowledge he wanted to show off by showing off that I knew a bloody sight more. It was competitive on both sides. I also realised that he was not quite like me. For one thing he was more organised, more conformist, more anxious to please his teachers than I had ever been. Perhaps I should have been more forthcoming. Jamie was a fine son. He donated blood and achieved a silver Duke of Edinburgh Award by way of a record breaking run through Epping Forest and several weeks of archery practice. He was courteous to just about everyone and even, occasionally, to me. His school encouraged him to aim for Oxford. Despite being raised on a London Council Estate by a single mum, he kept off drugs and out of trouble. What more could a father ask for?

I had hoped that one day, Jamie and his sister would wish to live with me, rather than their mother, but as they reached the age when they could make their wishes clear, it was clear that they preferred life in North London with their mother. Apart from my own selfish disappointment that I was not going to be a proper father, I felt that they would have done better attending school in Hertfordshire rather than Haringey. Ever since his mother insisted I pack up my bags and leave, it had been my dream to have the children live with me. At the time I was wheedling my parental responsibility, residence order and access through the courts, I was living on a narrow boat at Rickmansworth. Clair and Jamie were then aged five and four respectively; I can understand the court's reluctance to have them reside with me alongside the deep and dangerous waters of the Grand Union Canal. For a year after our settlement, the children did come to visit and sometimes stay longer on the good ship 'Violet Grace' and a couple of times Jamie did tumble into the pea green soup of rotten cats and rats' urine on which she floated. I plucked him out and he lived to tell the tale.

In 1995, with heartfelt thanks to the recession for depressing the price of property, I was able to borrow enough money to buy a flat above a shop. I recovered my furniture from the friends who had stored it for a couple of years and enjoyed a celebratory dinner with the children. Five years later, I was able to move on to a house. In the space of eight years I had moved from living in a van to owning my own house. I had taken on supply teaching work while fighting for custody of the children and it was the extra money obtained through this work that enabled me to pay my way, along with renting out spare rooms to tenants. Every weekend I collected them from their home and took them somewhere to have a good time - British Museum, Roman St Albans, Laser Shoot-out. Every year we went on holiday. I was often tired and always hard up, but I took my responsibilities seriously. Almost nothing was to hurt me more, in the aftermath of Jamie's Blue Mountain escapade than the fiction that I had 'walked out' on my son when he was three. Even more searing was Jamie's own disparagement of my twenty year struggle to be a decent father. I knew how I had juggled with time and money and Jean to do what I thought was best for my son and daughter. Maybe I ultimately became too involved and could not quite accept their graduation to independence and adulthood.

Jamie was indifferent to football. When he was about seven, he asked me who he should support. I told him to support his local team, which was Tottenham Hotspur. Unfortunately most of his peers preferred to follow the more successful team based a few miles further down the road. Spurs endured a dismal season under the dismal tutelage of Christian Gross, while their North London rivals jostled for the top of the table. Their supporters were not slow to sneer at Jamie's pathetic plastic reproduction of Darren 'Sick Note' Anderton. By the summer he had had enough.

"I'm not supporting Tott'nam anymore!"

I pleaded with him that this was not the way it worked. One day, maybe next season, maybe half a century from now, Spurs would bounce back.

"Look at me. Why don't I give up on England? Why don't I save myself year on year of pain by supporting Brazil instead? It's because you have to support the team you grow up with. It's like having a kid. No matter how crap they are to everyone else, even when even you know they're crap, you still love 'em!"

Perhaps I could have been more diplomatic. At least he didn't become an Arsenal fan. He just gave up on the beautiful game.

He went on to play rugby for the Borough of Haringey. Rugby is a game that baffles me. It is a game for middle-class boys.

One of our worst fall-outs took place on the day that England finally beat Germany in 2000. This was not the more recent and justly more celebrated game that ended 5-1 in England's favour. Like every other English bloke of my generation I had endured the dismal parade of penalty shoot-outs, goalkeeper gaffes, raised hopes and relentless under-achievement that stretched back over the thirty-four years since the last time England got to a final, let alone won it. How could a boy born in 1989 understand what it meant to me to see England take on the Jerries. He never picked up German expletives from a War Picture Library comic, never slid decals from a saucer of warm water onto the wings of an Airfix Spitfire, never read a Biggles book beneath the blankets by torchlight. He had been born into something called the European 'Community'. His Germans were 'economic partners', not those sinister, monocled scoundrels who do anything they are told, especially when blasting penalty shots past David Seaman. By half time, Jamie was bored. The score stood at 0-0. He insisted on watching Eddie Murphy on the other channel. It was his mum's house, so he controlled what went on the telly. I could only fulminate in impotent rage. My son was a milksop. Not fit to call himself Englishman. I stormed off to watch the second half down at 'The Spoons' in Colney Hatch Lane. It was there that a stranger hugged and kissed me. A fella, unfortunately. It was the joyous moment that Beckham's free-kick bounced onto the head of Alan Shearer and cannoned into the German goal. Jamie later said I acted in haste. Had I not stormed out, he would have let me watch the second half when the break was over. He was only having a laugh. There are some things which no Englishman can forgive. You don't mess about when England play the Jerries at footie, or the Argies for that matter. Or the Aussies at cricket.

I said he kept out of trouble. Except once.

One summer's eve Jean rang to say Jamie had been taken to Barnet Hospital with a cracked head. My teenage son had been showing off his self-certified tolerance of alcohol by swigging Southern Comfort in the kitchen of a girl he knew from school. When the ambulance came to scoop him off the pavement, where Jamie lay mired in his own blood, vomit and urine, he refused to co-operate.

"I can't go to 'ospital. I need to be in school tomorrow. Else I won't get to Oxford!"

This is not the usual response slurred out by tanked up, single-parented, cockney scrogs in the gutters of a North London council estate.

That's my boy!

When Jeff came back to England on his first visit since emigrating to Perth, he gave Jamie a book about Australia as a gift. It was Bill Bryson's *'Down Under'*. Jamie walked alongside his uncle as they climbed Ivinghoe Beacon together. Jeff told him Australia was a great place to live and invited my son to visit him there. Jamie was fifteen at the time but even then he was thinking about what he would do between school and university. He was impressed by what Jeff had to say about this land that filled its own continent.

I too thought it would be a good idea for him to go and work in Australia for a year. The West Australian economy was booming on the back of exports to China. A year spent wresting iron from the rusty hills of the Pilbarra or down the gold mines of Kalgoorlie, with black eyes gained from bar-room brawls between pulling nuggets like taters from the torrid plains of Double-u-a, would impress the ladies and look good on his cv. In the event, he got work in London to save up for the trip and it was to be a holiday rather than a work experience - a bit of fun before the serious business of further education and the rest of his life.

Chapter Three

The Journey

I was scheduled to do a day's teaching work the next day. I was reluctant to cancel at such short notice. It would also help take my mind off my missing son. Then there was the hope that he would be found on the Australian Wednesday as the search intensified. So I snatched a few hours' sleep and then drove down the motorway to North London.

I am one of those teachers who need the stimulus of a deadline to plan my lesson. For obvious reasons I had little to offer on this day. Luckily, the Year Threes were enjoying their week at a residential learning centre in the Brecon Beacons, so I had extra non-contact time and one less lesson to plan for in the time available. I had been asked to accompany the children on their trip to Wales and had been disappointed when it didn't work out due to the expense of employing me, as agency staff. In the event, it was a blessing that it worked out this way as it saved me the trouble of hurrying back from Wales and saved the school the trouble of sending someone else out to replace me.

Throughout the day I tried to focus on the needs of the children. I had told the staff about Jamie going missing so that they would realise why I was less jovial than usual. Kathy was in charge while the deputy head was away in Wales. She told me I could take time out from the lessons if I was unable to carry on. In fact it was only by concentrating on the children that I could put my boy's predicament to the back of my mind. This was to be the way I coped for the next eight days. Provided I was doing something I was okay. The worse times were when I was waiting around, frustrated that I wasn't actively doing something to get Jamie back. On duty in the playground, I wore a straw hat to shield me from the sun. It was mid-summer in Britain. I have always detested fair weather. I had no wish to suffer blisters on my bald patch. Beads of sweat trickled down my bonce like tiny spiders, tickling my skin. At least it was winter where I was going. The hat travelled to Australia with me and, after narrowly escaping confiscation as a prohibited item on entry to Australia, went on to become a kind of talisman. Three weeks later, tucked in among those blogs about my avarice, some toe-rag had the incredible cheek to have a pop at this inoffensive and practical item of apparel - "Cass in that silly hat.." (Tom of Bendigo).

"Slip, slap slop!" is an anti-skin-cancer mantra in Australia - intended to encourage slipping on a shirt, slapping on a hat and slopping on suncream. Cass was a living advert for that worthy cause. Call Cass a miserable, money-grubbing Pommy leech if you must, Tom, but leave the hat out of it, mate!

Of course, my efforts to keep occupied and try not to dwell on the situation were defeated by the kindness of those around me. The school was a special school in more ways than one. The staff were a kind and convivial community who knew me well. They wanted to commiserate and express good wishes for the safe return of my son. I felt obliged to tell them what little I knew and what I planned to do. There was no chance to forget Jamie's disappearance. During my time in New South Wales I received numerous text messages of support from staff at this school and I was touched by the delight they shared after my boy was found alive. They collected money for me. One of the sadder consequences of our falling out is that I never got to take him there to thank them.

After I finished teaching I used a school computer to search for a flight to Sydney and booked a flight leaving Heathrow at twelve noon the following day, arriving Sydney airport at midnight on Thursday. The flight was by Thai Airways with a short stopover in Bangkok. By the time I'd slept through the night, I would wake up in Australia on Friday morning. Having heard about Jamie at noon on Monday, it seemed strange that I would not be there to look for him until four days had passed. The flight takes almost a day to complete and, because of the time difference, you lose about ten hours of your life on arrival. I still thought it likely he would be found before I got there.

While I dawdled at the computer, I googled Jamie's name. The 'missing British backpacker' was pictured on a website operated by the New South Wales Police Service. I had seen the picture before, but only as a private e-mail attachment from Dallas Atkinson. It was a shock to see this poignant portrait on a publicly accessible news medium. His eyes sparkled with life. Would this picture be the last image of my beautiful boy?

On the way home, I stopped off at Muswell Hill to call on Jean. She was coping with the worry well, buoyed up by an unshakeable conviction that Jamie was too clever, too resourceful, not to come home to her. I borrowed a small backpack which was lying in the hallway. It belonged to Jamie. It would be useful to me when I went bushwalking to find him. I considered whether I ought to make the two hour drive up to Colchester to tell mum what was going on. Jamie is her only grandson and I knew that she would be devastated by the news. I decided it was for the best to leave it till I got back. If the news was good, she could savour it without having suffered the worry that preceded it. If the news was bad, at least she would enjoy a few more days of blissful ignorance. From a selfish point of view, I could do without the long drive there and back. I had a lot of things to do.

I drove back to Watford; stopping off at Tesco's to buy a holdall bag and a few other bits and pieces for my flight. Last time I went by plane, someone had tried to steal my bag from the luggage carousel. I had been nervous about challenging them as my bag was fairly commonplace, but I stepped up, unzipped the bag that they had placed on their trolley and saw that it was indeed mine. This time I would be sticking blue insulating tape all over the bag so that no one could make that kind of 'mistake' again. I had not eaten all day but now I forced myself to eat some rolls and bananas. I am diabetic and I was worried I might faint if I did not eat. Back at the house I broke the news to the two new tenants. They didn't seem to take it in. They had only known me for about a week. The news that their new landlord was rushing off to the other side of the world to search for a missing son probably sounded cinematic. Was I some kind of crazy fantasist? A few days later my face popped up on their TVs and on the front page of their papers. It was not what they expected when they moved in.

The internet is a wonderful thing and I simply cannot imagine how else I would have managed to book a hotel room and hire a van while sitting at my desk twelve thousand miles away from where they were waiting for me - all this in the middle of the night. I was even able to compare 'user comments' to avoid a room infested with bed-bugs in favour of a similarly priced clean one that 'felt like a prison'. I knew I would arrive around midnight so I wanted a place close to the airport, preferably within walking distance. I checked out maps and satellite images to see if this was feasible. The chosen hotel was within about twenty minutes' walk of the airport, alongside a Krispy Kreme doughnut emporium. This seemed a hopeful augury. Jamie is a devotee. I've told him he ought not to be scoffing doughnuts at all. When Jeff calls and I tell him I am heading for Australia, he says he will fly over from WA to meet up with me. I had been so wrapped up in my own worries that it had not occurred to me that he too would want to join the search for his nephew. I should have known that he wouldn't leave his kid brother alone at a time like this. We arrange to rendezvous at the Krispy Kreme at ten o'clock on Friday. I can't wait to tell Jamie that he has manoeuvred me into his favourite doughnut shop. I know he will be amused.

Another caller was Paul from the British High Commission. He asks if there is anything he can do for me. I am wary of this intervention. The last thing I need is some civil servant going through the motions of being nice to me - maybe offering me 'counseling' as if I had gone temporarily mad. The only help I wanted was anything that increased the chance of finding my son. Don't worry about me. I take the 'hope everything turns out okay' as read. The last thing I want is the sympathy of strangers. I prefer to deal with my emotions alone. Jeff had already spoken to them. They had been warned that I was not inclined to let them manage me I said thanks for the offer but I would be okay. In the event, Paul met me at the airport and saved me that twenty minute walk to the hotel.

After a night of little sleep I was up early to take my shower, load my bag and drive down the motorway to Jean's place. I couldn't find my favourite camera and so I took another one. I was to regret my haste as the substitute tended to let me down in Oz, and I lost some of the memories I might have recorded if the camera had been more cooperative. I was anxious to take pictures to bring home to Jean, so she could share the search with me. When I thought Jamie wasn't coming back, the pictures would serve to show that everything had been done to find him. I had bought a *'Daily Telegraph'*, so I could tackle the crossword to while away the time. I was shocked to see the Jamie/koala photograph and a report of 'missing British backpacker, Jamie Neale' on an inside page. I had not expected the story to be big news in the UK. Jamie is not the first kid to get lost on holiday. I knew my mum would be reading this paper and now regretted that I had not found time to see her. I was feeling queasy.

"Don't worry" said Jean, "We'll look after her". I knew mum too well to reckon she would submit to being looked after.

I kissed Clair's cheek as she lay in bed.

"I'm off to find your brother," I whispered.

These proved to be the last words I exchanged with Clair for a long time.

Then it was into Gary's car and off to the airport. Gary asked if he could come too. I wasn't keen. I was sure we'd argue if we were stuck together at such a stressful time. There was nothing to stop him making the trip by himself, but I preferred him to stay in London to look after Clair and Jean. I embraced him outside the Departure Terminal and then I was off on my own into a sea of strangers.

While I waited to be ushered through Airport Security I got the call on my mobile phone. My mother is too hard of hearing to use a normal phone so she subscribes to a service which transcribes the other speaker's words into text on a screen. Only one person can speak at any one time and there are formalities to be observed as the conversation flips between the two callers and the operator. This had the effect of transforming an emotive and intimate conversation between mother and son into a surreal, robotic three-way exchange of information. That I was standing in an echoing hall, swimming in a crowd of happy holiday makers all oblivious to my plight, made it all the more unbearable that my mother should have to learn about it like this.

"Tell me honestly, Andy... I've just been reading the Telegraph. Tell me, honestly. Is it our Jamie? Go Ahead."

"Mum, I'm so sorry. Yes, it is our Jamie. I didn't want to worry you. I'm at the airport now. I'm flying out to Australia to find him. Go Ahead".

My voice was quaking with emotion and there were tears in my eyes, but only the operator could hear me. There was a pause while the she typed out the words I had spoken and my mother read them.

"Okay... Look, don't worry about money. Just make sure you bring him back. You don't need to worry about me till you get back. Bye, love."

Then came the scouse accent of the operator.

"The other caller has cleared the line".

And that was that. I was alone with emotions of frustration and helplessness and love of my mum with her offer of money at a time when I was already worried about what this trip would cost. I could only line up here and sit down there and hand over tickets and passport, take off my belt and my keys and put them on again and then sit down and wait and wait among crowds of happy people who had no inkling of why I felt like this.

At last we boarded the plane, the staff welcoming the passengers with oriental gestures of politeness, palms pressed together and a bob of a bow. I wasn't sure whether I should be bobbing back. I was not in the mood to smile. Once the plane took off I felt a lot better. I could watch the progress of the flight on a screen, tracking our progress east over the Alps, Southern Russia and the Himalayas, heading for Thailand. Closer and closer. Hang on Jamie. Hang on. I'm on my way.

I was seated between a guy by the window who spoke no English and a brown-haired Irish lass. We started talking after we'd been sat next to each in silence for about six hours. She told me she had endured a twelve hour wait at Heathrow after her flight from Dublin had missed the connection. She was still not sure if she would be able to get an onward flight to Sydney when we got to Bangkok. This was why she had been too stressed out and grumpy to talk to me earlier. And maybe I looked like a sex tourist. I told her my story and showed her the picture in the *'Telegraph'*. After Jamie turned up again, she got my e-mail address from Sean Anderson and we exchanged messages for a while. Sarah was first to learn that I was calling this book 'Ruined Castle'. She stopped writing when things got kinda crazy: when I became a pariah.

Hour after hour, we inched across the face of the globe. I finished the crossword, which in its way was a kind of disappointment. It would have been good to let Jeff have a go at any clues that eluded me. We were different in a lot of ways but we liked to share a cryptic crossword, in a competitive sort of way. Does that make sense? I was not in the mood to watch *'Night at the Museum'*. I could only sit back and try every which way to arrange my legs in the space apportioned to me. I couldn't sleep, though my watch showed it was the middle of the night back home.

Bangkok from the air is an arrangement of rectangles. All the streets seem to meet at right angles and all the fields and ponds and paddy fields are rigidly quadrilateral. It's like a looking down on a Mondrian without the primary colours. Our aeroplane landed so smoothly that some of the passengers gave the pilot a spontaneous round of applause. I liked Thai Air. They seemed laid back and nice.

As I chugged along the travelators to find my onward flight to Sydney, I phoned home to see if Jamie had been found. No news. This was getting serious. He had been out there for six nights. They had been searching for him for three of them.

After an hour's wait I was back in the big blue sky again, gazing down on the dark green islands and lazy meandering rivers of Indonesia, then the sea was gone and we were flying over the riven red heart of Australia. Sarah waved to me from a couple of seats away. I was pleased she had got a seat, astonished it was so close to mine. Night overtook us as we neared our destination. Soon all I could see were spangles of light from the occasional town or gas station. There was a lump in my heart when the screen showed we were flying over the Blue Mountains. If my son was there he might look up and see the lights of the plane, I thought. But then I realised it was raining as we dropped through the clouds and came in to land, nearer one o'clock than midnight.

My companion for this part of the journey was a big, likeable Pakistani man in a shirt and tie. Unlike Sarah, he introduced himself as soon as he sat down. I was the first native English speaker he'd ever met and this was the first time he'd left his own native land. He was planning to meet a brother living in Adelaide. We got on well and, when I showed him Jamie's picture, he said there was a prayer in the Qur'an for people who are lost or in peril. He would pray for us and I would get my son back, *inshallah!* I was so desperate for any kind of help that I was tempted to make a deal with Allah - bring back my son and I will turn Muslim. I held back. I knew I was too fond of beer and sausages not to relapse when the pressure was off.

It is better not to make a promise than to break it. I remain thankful to Mr Chaudhry for his prayer. I will also thank Allah, if ever we should meet.

We got on too well for our own good in fact. He asked me to stick by him as we proceeded through the complications of admission to Australia. He found colloquial language difficult to comprehend and the various procedures baffling. I was happy to help if he would ask his brother to drop me off at my hotel. We ended up trundling our bags together on the same luggage trolley. This was after I had stopped him from placing his hand luggage on the carousel. He thought it was just another security check rather than the place you got your own luggage back! The sight of this smartly dressed Pakistani man sharing his trolley with that scruffy white bloke in the straw hat was too much for Aussie officialdom.

We were pulled over to be searched and questioned with a thoroughness that made it clear that they did not believe a word I said about having just met the guy on the plane. I showed them the newspaper picture of Jamie. Maybe I was lying, using the news story as smokescreen to smuggle a kilo or two of Afghan opiates into the country. We didn't even have the same surname. At one point I thought they were going to impound my hat. All items made from wood or straw, along with any kind of food, are prohibited from entry to Australia. After about half an hour's delay and the perfunctory groin sniff of a cocker spaniel, I was permitted to proceed. They even let me keep the hat. The chubby lady said she would look out for Jamie went she went bushwalking next weekend.

"Find that boy and I'll marry you!" I replied. I meant it too.

A flustered Mr Chaudhry was still being grilled by the guys in pale blue shirts. I tried to say goodbye but they ushered me away. In the land that invented the boomerang it sometimes seems that every well-meant gesture comes whirling back to smack someone in the face.

As I went through the door into the night outside, I was looking out for Mr Chaudhry's brother, just to let him know the guy was nearly through, but I was distracted by the sight of a man holding up a card printed with my name.

"I'm Richard Cass".

"How do you do? I'm Paul from the British High Commission".

Paul was a dapper, bespectacled chap with a slight North Country accent. I was grateful to get a lift to my hotel as it was now almost two o'clock in the morning. We found the Krispy Kreme and then we found the hotel.

It was easy to see why that user-reviewer had described staying at the Hotel Formule 1 (sic) as like paying to go to prison. The room was sparsely furnished with TV, digital clock radio and two iron bedsteads. The en-suite bathroom had a dimply, rubberised floor and a plughole in the middle, but the place was clean and surprisingly well-insulated against the noise of the nearby airport. I slept well enough in the circumstances and I was content to come back the following week.

It was raining and rather cold. I thought about Jamie as I slipped between the cool white sheets.

Chapter Four

The Old Man

'The Tower' is one of the major arcana in a standard pack of Tarot cards. 'New Age' mysticism has thrown up pack designs a-plenty to tempt the modern prophetess but I find them, for the most part, garish and over fussy. None can stand comparison with the plain, picture-book quality of a pack designed in the early years of the twentieth century by Pamela Coleman-Smith to accompany a book by the occultist and founder of The Order of the Golden Dawn, A.E. Waite. It remains the most popular deck in use in the English speaking world to this day.

This deck features 'The Tower' rent by a single jagged stroke of lightning, as two figures, man and woman, tumble slack-jawed into the night. Flames explode from the tower's roof and windows. The falling figures seem suddenly rent from familiar comforts by this unlooked for ruination of their castle. Bewildered and taken unawares, they tumble to destruction.

Jamie's adventure is eerily mirrored in this pack of cards. He was last seen, of course, at the 'Ruined Castle' rock formation. The card of 'The Fool' shows a young wandervogel, pack over his shoulder, poised to step across the edge of a precipice. Eyes are raised to beyond the horizon and in his right hand he holds a plucked rose. A little dog yaps desperately at the young man's feet, but the strolling fool remains oblivious to the peril ahead. This was my son. After a long week of desperate searching, I truly believed that he had stepped off into that void. Maybe he had leant out to take a photograph, maybe simply crashed on through darkening bush and failed to heed that dizzy perpendicularity until it was too late. Maybe he leaned over to experience the thrill, misjudged his balance and fell.

There is a card of 'Death' and a card for 'The Devil' and Kings of Coins and Staves and other such stuff. There is even a card for the old man who came looking for this boy who stepped off the rocks of 'Ruined Castle' to disappear off the face of the earth - a bit like those pretty young things at 'Hanging Rock'. But that, of course, was a fiction. The fool had spoken to the couple who last saw him there. Told them he was on his way to Solitary. "He wore a Prada t-shirt", they said.

"The numbskull wears Prada", I'd quipped, a few months earlier, when Jamie was safe in the Five Bells pub in Finchley. My surname is reckoned to be a medieval contraction of 'Cassandra', cant name for a prophetess.

'The Hermit' is a cowled, bearded old man, who walks with the aid of a staff. In his right hand he holds a lantern. Apart from the monkish garb, he could be that ancient Cynic philosopher, Diogenes of Synope. Diogenes proclaimed that happiness is an inward boon, independent of wealth or comfort. He is supposed to have either dressed or slept in a storage jar and begged for his sustenance. He then went out into the market place of Athens with a lighted lamp while the sun shone bright. 'To search for an honest man', he said. The Hermit depicted in the Rider-Waite tarot pack does not wander the agora of Athens in search of honest men. He seems to stand alone atop a cold mountain peak with snow beneath his feet. Similar peaks feature in the background to the same pack's image of 'The Fool.

Of course, I have not always been this bearded old hermit. Once upon a time, I was young. My own youthful wanderings took me to Ireland and Scotland and France and the streets of seventies London. By the standards of the time, and indeed by the examples of my son and my father, this was hardly worthy of the name of travel. I had little money when I was a young man and preferred to spend the little I had on cars rather than inconvenience. Having travelled by sea from Melbourne to Tilbury Docks in my first year of life, stopping off at Aden, Port Said and the ruins of Pompeii on the way, it was not till 2002 that I returned to take a look at the land where I was born. This time, I travelled by way of Singapore Airport and a Boeing 747. Jamie warned me, before I flew, to look out for spiders in my shoes. I suffered from nothing worse than an ant bite and the stewardess who insisted I mustn't look out the window at the early morning sunlight lighting up the mountains of Afghanistan. People are trying to sleep, Sir. Close the blind, Sir.

I still kick the telly when those ladies blind me with lip-gloss and tell me they're a great way to fly.

Jeff was fifty years old when I came to visit. We were in our thirties when we'd last met. Jeff's two older girls had both left school and I'd never met my youngest niece before. They were Australians now, by speech and passport. Jeff is twenty-seven months older than me, but he still made it to the top of Bluff Knoll Mountain about twenty minutes before I got there. "Did you see that king snake by the side of the track?" he asked.

"Thanks for not waiting for me, brother. I could have sat on the bloody thing!"

Insouciance in the face of high altitude peril is integral to our genes.

Jeff has always been fitter than me. As a teenager I suffered the slings and arrows of disbelieving kids who questioned our fraternity - "Are you really Jeff's brother?" – so vast appeared the disparity between Jeff's athleticism and mine, between his footballing prowess and my kick and rush. I was actually a reasonable goalkeeper but shared school and birth cohort with England prospect, Mervyn Day. No wonder I turned to books for solace.

We were raised in a land of *Bird's* Custard.

England in the sixties was a land of Hillman Imps and Riley Elves, Zephyrs and Zodiacs and men on strike. There was carpet of quality-you-can-afford and sweets made-to-make-your-mouth-water. England had just won the war and would go on to win the World Cup. There was wrestling on the telly on Saturday afternoon and Captain Pugwash and Doctor Who. Blue Peter happened every Monday. All in various shades of grey. We read *'Beano'* and *'Topper'* and *'Valiant'* which we got in big bundles when other kids' mothers chucked them out. If we were lucky, we got hold of *'Superman'* and *'Green Lantern'* and, sometimes, more scary American magazines with titles like *'Creepy Worlds'* and *'Strange Tales'*. When the old man was out at work we played Radio Caroline. The rest of the time we put up with the Home Service. We played outside till the sun went down, whatever the weather. We got into fights and smashed up empty houses for fun. We nicked things without flicker of conscience, collected birds' eggs with the same half-cock dilettantism we expended on dinky toys and *Brook Bond* tea-cards. This was all normal behaviour for boy children then and, so far as I knew, no-one thought any the worse of us for it. We were not delinquent or feral or a social problem. We were kids.

It was the best of times to be young. Parents and grandparents survived war and economic depression, post-war austerity and tin baths. We had free, full-fat milk at school and free bottled orange syrup for my baby sisters. We also got free pricks in the arm to stop us getting paralysed by polio. Measles and chicken pox came and went, leaving scars that eventually faded away. Most amazing of all was that my mum got free money from the Post Office every week. Just for having kids! Had any generation in the whole history of the world ever been so cosseted before?

It was just as well that this benign Labour government was committed to mass bribery of the electorate, for our old man was a miser who resented every penny wasted upon the sons he'd spawned. His bread was spread with *'Kangaroo'* branded butter, while we made do with *'Stork'* margarine. The rest of the family might sit down to a different, less appetising dinner than that put before our lord and progenitor.

"Australians have so much meat, they won't condescend to dine on offal," explained our mum. Fine for the missus and kids though!

In the early sixties, we were too poor to afford holidays or fridge or phone; expenditure which most of my classmates took for granted. My mate, Terry, not only had a fridge but there was a bottle of *Suncrush* orange squash inside it. I watched him pour himself a glass without even having to ask his mum - affluence beyond my imaginings! Another gulf, of which I was painfully conscious at the time, was the way all the other kids had birthday parties and invited their mates to come along. We went along to these parties but never reciprocated. We did get cake and candles with each passing year, supplemented by sandwiches and boiled eggs instead of jelly and platefuls of *'Penguin'* chocolate bars. I was ever the Cinderella so far as birthday cake was concerned. One year, mum could only afford a home baked *'Viota'* sponge, interlarded with a smudge of *'Stork'* margarine beaten up with icing sugar. She stuck those little silver balls on top, onto the bare brown crust. What did I expect, being born so soon after Christmas? Now I'm kinda grown up, I realise how hard she had it with the old man and money.

Pocket money - taken for granted by most of my mates - never entered our income stream, though we got the odd penny out of the change from fetching mum's fags from the shop. Jeff and I sang carols door to door in December, collected for the guy in November and picked peas in July. Then there were bottles. In those far off days, you got a few pence back from the shop when you returned the empties. We collected the bottles of drinkers too lazy or flush with cash to bother and organised raids on a local sports and social club to nick empties from the crates out back. We spent our wealth on salted crisps, blackjack chews and sweets designed to look like glowing cigarettes. We never got fat.

On the subject of money, the cynics (pace Diogenes!) will be gratified to learn that I earned my headmaster's plaudit for being the only boy in the class who could recite the script on a pound note from memory:

"I promise to pay the bearer, on demand…"

"By Jove, he's got it!" chuckled jolly Mr Gregory, in what was probably a parody of Professor Higgins that went over my head at the time. This was not intimation of my future cupidity, more evidence of my thrill for poetic language.

I went on to be one of only two kids in my year that passed their eleven plus exam. Mum bought me a 'Picnic' chocolate bar as reward. The other kid got a new bicycle. Misery memoir or what?

We were mildly slapped around by mum and dad, but no more than most of the other kids at the time. At this time, it was widely believed that God had gifted children with thicker hair than their parents so the little sods could be held fast while shaken to express timely wrath whenever they swore or stole. Mum resorted to taking my library cards away as punishment for stealing a book I couldn't bear to take back. I forged the old man's signature and rejoined. I had to hide my borrowed books for months, like samizdat from the KGB. Mum found them of course, but let me keep the forged library cards.

We almost never went out as a family group, which bothered us not one jot and we were expected to help around the house, which bothered us quite a lot. My favourite job was gathering kindling wood for the living-room fire and splitting it into bits with a garden spade. The worst job was reserved for Sunday afternoons, when gales of laughter mocked Jeff and me from the wireless; laughing at Jimmy Clitheroe in actual fact, but it still felt like it was us. Every bloody Sunday we all sat down to a lunch of New Zealand lamb incinerated alongside roast potatoes. It was almost the only unprocessed meat we ever ate, though we might glimpse cuts of prime steak disappearing down Poppa's throat during the other days of the week. The meat on our plates was mostly grease and gristle but it was what was left in the baking tray that caused my brother and me most grief. Such was the tenacity with which the remnants of those slaughtered lambs clung to the tray whereupon they had recently been cremated that I reckon they must be bottle feeding them on *Bostik* back home on those grassy southern plains. These greasy encrustations defied every assault of steel wool, elbow grease and Ajax powder. Even now I cannot eat lamb, unless it's decently attired behind pitta bread and hot chilli sauce.

Any man or woman born in Britain in the fifties will recognise elements of this reminiscence of childhood in the early sixties. Any person born since about 1980 will probably find the sketch about as remote from their own experience as the life story of a child born in pre-Columbian Peru. There was yet another difference between then and now. We knew what cold weather looked and felt like. On winter mornings, we woke in our unheated bedroom to the sight of ice-patterns etched across single-glazed window panes. I know of nothing so strange and beautiful as this depiction of ferny foliage formed by the simple action of sub-zero temperature on molecules of hydrogen oxide. I count it - along with coincidental relative size of sun and moon, the contemporaneous occurrence of both blue whales and humans and the Africa/India shaped ears of elephants living in each of these two places - as proof positive for the existence of a divine comedian.

I remember, with pleasure, the great freeze of '63. The snow stood stacked in rock hard slush piles for three whole months. I remember the thaw as I wandered, lonely as an eight year old, up the road to One Tree Hill. The trickle of water all around and steam whisping up from a black, tarmacadamed road, still mottled with crusts of compacted snow.

Oh to be in England, then.

The part of old England where the foregoing fun and games played out from about 1960 till 1966 was a small town on the northern shore of the Thames Estuary. I remember the place with much affection, as, I suppose, most people do who look back on their early years without too much reason to be uncheerful. Stanford-le-hope is known locally as 'Stanf'd-lee-yope', with stress on the first and third syllables. When I lived there, every family seemed to be Cockneys from West Ham. The East End local councils had built estates in Essex to accommodate their surplus blitzed-out population.

I was unusual in that I was born in Australia and I got teased about this at school - 'Andrew the Kangaroo'. Now that I've sort of grown up, I choose to be known by my middle name. I cringe every time my mother calls me 'Andy'. The other time my antipodean birth became an issue was the way any backyard cricket match played out between me and Jeff got talked up as a clash between England and the Aussies. England always won. Halcyon days.

In the year of sixty-six, we moved from Cockney south Essex to a dismal village on the outskirts of Chelmsford. I was eleven and therefore about to enter secondary school.

Shortly before my father passed away, I asked him what had prompted him to make a move which brought nothing but misery to me for the next eight years. What had induced him to exchange the vista from his bedroom window - the gleaming towers of Coryton oil refinery, stately tankers gliding to and fro before a distant prospect of the hop-fields of Kent - for that view of the back end of a *Buxted* Chicken Shack?

"It made me feel cold", he whimpered. "All that cold grey water. I never felt warm in this country, not since Rose made us come back from Australia".

I suddenly realised how seldom I had seen this man without a jumper or a cardigan or a dressing gown on, and forever toasting his bum cheeks against the open fire.

I spent my early teens in fights with the local kids. I had never gone to junior school with these brats and, as none of them had the brains to pass their eleven plus exams, I didn't get to know them at my grammar school either. Even worse was that I went about four years without having meaningful conversation with any girl of similar age to mine, apart from my sisters. There were no girls at King Edward VI Grammar School - for boys. The boys I met there were not like me. They were posher, more at ease with adults and more middle-class. I cannot claim to be anything other than middle-class myself. My family was no longer shacked up in a unit on a hillside in Melbourne, with paraffin for cooking and lighting. My father worked behind a desk and he was buying his own house on a mortgage. But I was an oik in the eyes of many classmates and even in the judgment of some teachers. I seemed scruffy and penniless through my father's penny-pinching ways. Even worse, I spoke what is today labeled 'Estuary English'. I dropped me aitches and still use 'me' as possessive pronoun. Now I've moved on, 'Estuary English' has become hip, classless and yoof-ful. It was certainly not considered so in the county town of Essex in 1967. It meant you was 'fick'.

"I don't know how you got into Transitus", sneered my biology mistress to the rest of the top stream. "Maybe you were good at woodwork". Cue laughter. At the most recent biology exam, I'd come third out of a hundred kids. I was also pretty good at woodwork.

As those awful teenage years passed by, I did fall behind my classmates and began to play truant. It was easy enough to fake an absence note from my father as he never wrote anything to the school for them to compare it with. Nor did we possess a phone to catch me out by. I may have simply fulfilled the school's low expectations of a cockney scruff, but I also had things going on at home, where the old man regularly drank himself into a frenzy of suspicion and Catholic religious mania. Jeff bore the brunt of this tedious pugnacity. He was tall and athletic and beloved by his mother. By the time he was studying for his 'A' levels, he had moved into digs, paid for by his mother.

Of course, the work was getting harder too. At junior school I was clever enough to work out what had to be done without needing to be told by the teacher. Once I got into the top stream of the grammar school, natural cleverness no longer sufficed. My classmates not only had ability, but they also listened to what the teacher said. I struggled in Latin, French and Maths. So long as the work involved writing in English, I could get by. As with any kid at school, there were teachers I liked, teachers I feared and teachers I messed around. I messed around in maths.

I did not kiss a girl till I got to be seventeen. The singular circumstances that attended this episode have, for me at least, taken on an epic quality with consequences cascading down the decades like the shiny apple of discord tossed among the gods of Olympus that set in train the Siege of Troy. Patricia was a willowy, plain-faced sixteen year old who stacked the shelves of *Sainsbury's* at weekends. I stacked alongside her. After much prompting from a friendly old woman co-worker, I asked her out and we went to a fair together. I was surprised and delighted that she did not recoil in horror when I slipped a hand inside her blouse as we kissed. As we walked back to her house, an irate old man could be discerned striding purposefully towards us.

"Come round Sunday," she hissed. "My parents will be away".

"I can't!" I replied. "I've got to revise Biology 'A' level".

The purposeful strider grabbed Patricia and impelled her towards the house.

"Get in!" he snarled. He did not look at me.

The Olympian Apple of Discord was claimed by three goddesses - Hera, Athena and Aphrodite. Their dispute was resolved by the celebrated 'Judgment of Paris'. Paris, prince of Troy, was out minding sheep on a mountainside when called to adjudicate their dispute and award the apple, mischievously labeled *'to the fairest'*. Paris was offered the conquest of Asia as a douceur by Hera, for she was a warrior goddess. Athena was goddess of wisdom and therefore offered Paris the chance to be the wisest mortal that ever breathed if only she were chosen. But Aphrodite, goddess of love, offered Paris the passion of Helen, the most sexy woman in the world, if Paris handed the apple to her. Paris chose love. He thereby also chose to lose a war and to be unwise. Neither Hera nor Athena could forgive the snub they suffered. So far as was in their particular power, they aided the enemies of Paris, Helen and Troy. After ten years of siege the war was lost and Troy destroyed. The goddess of wisdom so dulled the wits of the Trojans that they trundled the wooden horse through unbroken gates into the heart of their city. Still, Paris had made the best choice. For ten wonderful years he had wallowed in the bed of the lovely Helen. I chose Athena.

I had turned down a chance to be initiated into the delights of real, bare-naked, three-dimensional sex while Patricia's mum and dad were away. I had chosen to revise my Biology 'A' level. I got a grade E, so even choosing Athena over Aphrodite didn't make me all that wise in the short term. As for Aphrodite, boy did she get her own back for that stupid abstention! The bitch condemned me to a lifetime of misery, mischance and misapprehension in all things appertaining to the pursuit of love. Opportunities to run ladies home were to be dashed by flat car batteries and lost keys. Seductions might be interrupted by unannounced other lovers, attacks by ravenous hamsters or interminable phone calls from the lady's mother - all this throughout those years when blood was a-throbbing with great gobs of testosterone.

As for Patricia, she dumped me before I got any second chance. My boast to work colleagues about fondling her breasts seems to have upset her for some reason. I had to wait another three long, hormonally driven years to find some other girl mad enough to have sex with me. I probably, could have got there sooner - I was not too bad looking at this time - but six years Trappist seclusion in an all-boy grammar school, interspersed with six years sojourn in the village of the damned had left me tongue tied and bashful in direct relation to the attractions of any female who approached me. I call it 'The Curse of Aphrodite'. Nor did Mamma help much when she assured me that girls feel dirty and humiliated by sex. They put up with it because they love you, so it's a good idea to get it over with quickly. Thanks for that, mum. And thanks from Jane, Pauline and Christine too.

I came to live in London soon after I left school. I tried to get into a polytechnic to study Anthropology but my ex-Headmaster, quote, 'hesitated to recommend me'. I took an 'A' level in English Literature while working full time. I was surprised to get an 'A' grade. In those days 'A' grades meant you were really, really clever. I ended up studying English at Leeds University when I got to twenty-five. English all on its own seemed like too much of a good thing so I combined it with philosophy which sounded interesting and impressive. I was soon astonished to find that I was cleverer than almost all the other undergraduates. I was awarded the Harvey Prize for philosophy in my first year and the Crabtree Prize for brilliance in first year exams - or something like that. This was the first time anything as extraordinary as this had happened to me since Mr Gregory heard me recite the script off a pound note without looking. So, in the end, Athena came good.

In the seven years between leaving school and going to Leeds, I did enjoy two blissful years in the arms of Irenka. Irenka fell in love with me after I met her in a nightclub in Bayswater, West London. After a few months of intense carnality, I realised I loved her too. I asked her to marry me and she said 'yes' and blubbed her eyes out as we lay naked together in my single bed with a bottle of Matteus Rosé. Although she had been born in England, her parents had escaped from Hungary during the 1956 uprising. She was therefore deliciously exotic to me and I loved to hear her gabble away in her incomprehensible mother tongue to other émigrés. She had masses of dark red hair and a lovely, chubby body. She would pin back her dress when we went clubbing or partying to maximise the extent of cleavage on show without actually popping out her nipples. Wow...! This was a woman who actually enjoyed sex, ripping off my clothes rather than the other way round. We went to a lot of weddings together, including Jeff's, and people said, "You'll be next!", but I thought it would be best to get my degree sorted first. Athena trumps Aphrodite.

In 1980, the DJ at the club where we met played Neilson's *'Can't live, if living is without you'* as we danced in each other's arms "because Rick's off to university, leaving Irenka in London all alone".

In January of the following year, she wrote to say it was over between us. She had met someone else. I was heartbroken but by now I appreciated that it was hard for a woman to love from afar. How could I compete with someone who was on the spot while I was two hundred miles away? I still hoped we could get back together when I'd done my three years in Leeds and came back to live in London. Seven months later, I got a call from a good friend of mine to say Irenka had been murdered. She was found asphyxiated in the flat of Jonny Dean. Jonny was the DJ who had played Neilson's *'Can't live, if living is without you'* as we danced the previous September. Irenka had gone out with him for a couple of months then tried to break away. He became a jerk, obsessively phoning, begging, writing notes and turning up to badger her. She agreed to go out with him just once more if he agreed to leave her alone. He took her to a restaurant where even the waiters were induced to plead on his behalf, then took her back to his place and killed her. I am grateful for just one mote of comfort in this awful tragedy. Jonny Dean hanged himself on the night he murdered the woman I loved. Otherwise I would be in gaol today for stalking and killing him.

Twenty eight years later, as I sat down in a police interview room in Katoomba to be told my son was probably dead and could I please submit a sample of DNA in case they someday find a maggoty ribcage that may be his, I remembered Irenka and demanded of God what I had done to deserve this second loss of someone I loved so much.

Numb with grief, I coped by avoiding anything that reminded me of my lost love. I could not even buy a pair of leather boots when I noticed they were made in Hungary. I completed my three years at Leeds and went on to teacher training. The road untaken was the A23 down to Brighton, where I was offered a chance to do a Master's Degree in Critical Theory, hopefully leading up to a Doctorate. In London I enjoyed cheap digs in wonderful West Hampstead and I had a girlfriend. In 1984, teacher training prospects were required to spend a couple of weeks assisting in a primary school before starting their college course. I enjoyed one of those rare, balmy days when the children are so delightful and the task of educating them such a doddle. I was only an assistant and the class teacher was very good. I phoned the British Academy and said I would not be needing their grant. Next day I was left alone with the kids for a short while and realised what a big mistake I'd made. Oh and the girlfriend sodded off back to Fife. Thanks, Aphrodite.

After a year at the British Institute of Education, where my reservations about the role of radical feminism as driver-up of standards in basic literacy led me to be unpopular with my tutors and some fellow students, I ended up teaching English at a secondary school in the East End of London. During term time I had no time for a social life, no time to read anything that wasn't directly related to my teaching work and no time for sleep. The kids were awful, though I was aware that most of my colleagues seemed to cope better than me, despite my hard work. It was me. I was a lousy teacher. By this time, I had moved in with Jean, Jamie's future mother. I told her I was quitting the teaching job to write a book. One of the joys of teaching in the summer of '86 consisted in removing frozen drinks from the boys and lining them up on a high shelf over the blackboard. A half sucked jubbly is a thing of beauty. The colouring lingers in the heart of the ice, glowing like some huge exotic jewel through the frostiness of the depleted outer layers. Some of these jubblies were a lovely shade of blue. I worked as a security guard while I wrote the book. It was a job I'd done in my student days. 'Blue Jubbly' was a 'strong and original book... worthy of publication' said Hutchinsons, the publishers. It was just that they weren't taking anything on at the moment. Neither was anyone else. Not my book anyway.

By this time I had two kids to support. After I broke up with Jean, I returned to teaching. I knew supply teaching could be hell, but I thought it would help with getting the court order for the children to reside with me if I didn't have to work in the school holidays. This time round I was mostly teaching younger children. I was still a lousy teacher or, at any rate, a lousy disciplinarian. But the job wasn't as bad as I expected and I got plenty of work. I carried on with the security work too, kind of planning another book but never getting the time. I was going to write a semi-biography set in a parallel universe entitled *'I was Alan Titchmarsh's Arse Double'*. It was to be a study in sublime under-achievement. Two incomes brought me enough to buy a flat and then a house, support two kids and take them on holiday. So it went on for year after year. The children grew older and taller while my beard grew greyer and my belly got fatter. Sometimes I'd drive bleary eyed from one job to the other, changing clothes on the way. I drank a lot of coffee. It would all be worth it when the children came to live with me.

Eventually I found a niche teaching children with severe learning difficulties at a school in North London. Both staff and children were fantastic and they liked me back. I took on a bit of a timetable along with plenty of supply work. I taught RE with lots of dressing up. Experiences and encounters were important for these children, some of whom could communicate only by nods, glances or smiles. I dressed as Wurzel Gummidge for the Harvest Festival, Rabbi Richard and Buddhist monk. I bought a Santa suit for Christmas. I fell in love with that school. I was actually enjoying my teaching work.

In 2009, the deputy head asked me if I could accompany a group of children on their trip to Pendarren in the Brecon Beacons. I was agreeable but, in the event, I did not go because my agency wanted too much for my being on duty out of hours. This was to prove fortunate. Otherwise I would have been stuck in Old South Wales when I got the call about Jamie in New South Wales.

Chapter Five

The Chopper

On my first morning in Oz, I ate cereal and drank coffee downstairs. A copy of Sydney's *'Daily Telegraph'* was on the newspaper rack with the big picture of James and the giant koala on the front cover. I was tempted to tell everyone that I was the father and I'd just flown twelve thousand miles to find him, but I didn't want to be seen to be showing off or milking sympathy or seeking attention. The hotel was busy with low-budget travellers. I seemed to be the only one on my own. No one took a blind bit of notice of this old man reading the paper with his son on the front cover and the haunted look on the old man's face.

The first task of the morning was to collect the Toyota Hiace van I'd booked over the internet. At this time, I had not made any arrangements for accommodation in Katoomba. I was worried how much the trip was costing me and thought, as a last resort, I might buy a sleeping bag and sleep in the back of the van. At the time, I had no anticipation that I would be hounded by news reporters when I got to Katoomba. It took about fifteen minutes to walk to the depot where I was to collect the vehicle. Then I had to wait another twenty before the first staff arrived to hand it over. I showed my documents and signed a promise to pay all motorway tolls or risk having penalty charges put on my credit card. Then I was behind the wheel, feeling much better to be independently mobile again. The fact that there were three seats in the front seemed a good omen - Jeff, Jamie and me. The diesel engine purred like a jungle cat as I drove off, then wipers juddered across the screen when I flicked to indicate a left turn. It took three days to get used to the stalks being opposite to those I was used to back home. The rain had blown over and the sun was shimmering on the last puddles as I drove back to the hotel to collect my bags and check out. Like Paul the night before, I drove past the hotel on the opposite side of the perimeter road and had to go miles before I could turn round and come back. I now had a van at my disposal and my son was only seventy miles away. All I had to do was drive west and find him. Things were progressing to plan.

I took a call from Jeff. He was stuck in Perth as he'd booked his flight for the wrong day. He'd even turned up at the airport to be told he was twenty-four hours too early. He was irritated and apologetic that he'd screwed up at such a stressful time for the two of us. I would have to drive to the mountains on my own and he would follow me up by train. There wasn't going to be any talismanic rendezvous at Krispy Kreme after all.

How difficult could it be to drive up from Sydney to that world class tourist destination of the Blue Mountains? Must be signposted all the way from Cape York to Macquarie Island. I even found out the names of a couple of towns along the Great Western Highway. Just follow the road signs.

I began by heading into the centre of the city through the morning rush. There were plenty of signs but not for anywhere I recognised as somewhere I needed to go. I even found myself driving across the iconic coat hanger, gawping at 'that other Taj Mahal' over on Bennelong Point. I had read a book about the building of Sydney Opera House. I lived in hopes of being asked to name the architect in a pub quiz sometime. Joern Utzon had been a difficult man, broken by his sojourn in New South Wales. When I finally got to ogle his creation, in the flesh so to speak, Utzon had been dead for just four months. I only wish I had more time to linger. I did not know it, but I was going the wrong way. I gave up looking for direction signs and tried to steer by the bright morning sun. It was getting on for nine in the morning so I knew I had to head away from the sun to make my way west, but every road I took seemed to take me round a bend. Progress west was perceptible but came in fits and starts. There were plenty of signs to suburbs I'd never heard of but nothing to direct me to the places I'd memorised. In a place called West Ryde I stopped to ask directions from a guy fixing a telephone sub-station. I told him I had to get to the Blue Mountains to find my lost son.

"Strewth! Hope yer find 'im, mate!"

At least I could be sure I was still in Australia.

He gave me such a ridiculously complicated set of directions that I forgot which way to go as soon as I got back in the van. Luckily, I had heard him mention 'Paramatta'. So now I knew which suburb to head for. Even when I did come up against the Great Western Highway, I had to shout across to another van driver to find out which way to go.

"Go right!"

I was finding Australia an easy place to get lost in.

After an hour of triple carriageway and frequent traffic lights, the road narrows to two lanes as it writhes back and forth up into the hill country. A railway line tags along for the ride, following the same historic route across the Great Dividing Range. This track had been blazed by three settlers in 1812. Blaxland, Lawson and Wentworth had worked out that it was better to follow the ridge than the river valleys. The rivers all lead to impassable waterfalls. For these travellers, the mountains were no place to linger. While England had come to appreciate the Romantic allure of the picturesque and the sublime, it was the prospect of 'champagne' country beyond the mountains that inspired their expedition. Wentworth had an ear for portentous rhetoric: *'Till nearer seen the beauteous landscape grew, op'ning like Canaan on rapt Israel's view'*. The original road was built by convict labour in 1815, op'ning up the interior to white blokes and their sheep. Not such good news for the black fellows.

As I reached the outskirts of Katoomba, an ambulance came speeding the other way with its lights flashing. That'll be him, I rejoiced. They've found him.

At Katoomba I parked up the van and walked up the High Street asking for the Police Station. It was a shabbily picturesque sort of place. A bit like a memory of provincial England in the sixties with chapels and owner-occupied shops and astonishingly quiet - no music blaring from any direction. The locals were all swaddled in their quilted anoraks while I sweated profusely in a blue and white polo shirt. I found Katoomba Police Station and asked to see Dallas Atkinson. He wasn't there. Jamie was still missing. Everyone was up at the search base camp. An officer who introduced himself as Mick Bostock offered to drive me up there. I explained about my van being parked at the other end of town and said I'd be back in twenty minutes. As I walked out I was politely accosted by a guy who looked like a roadie for a seventies rock band. He asked if I had any words for the Telegraph. This was a bit of a surprise.

"I'm sorry. I'm busy now. Maybe later".

I saw this guy many times over the next few days. I became quite fond of him and even tried to give him an interview by phoning a name and number I'd been given, but the name I thought was his turned out to be someone else's and they got the story instead. His appearance was the first penny raindrop of that deluge of media interest that was waiting to engulf me.

I went next door to the Youth Hostel where Jamie had spent his last night before heading out on his walk. As soon as I introduced myself, the lady in the kiosk burst into tears and said "I need to give you a hug".

We hugged. She went to fetch her boss. I got another hug. I collected the same rudimentary map of the route to Mount Solitary that my son had taken then headed back to get the van.

I was thirsty, having dined on lime and chilli tortilla chips at a gas station outside Penrith. It is surprisingly difficult to find a bar in Katoomba, but I eventually came across a restaurant that served alcohol and tried to order a beer.

"Can I have a semi? Or a midi or something? Of Lager?"

The barman looked at me in bewilderment. I was trying to recollect a word I'd been taught by Jeff when drinking at a West Australian bar seven years before. The word turned out to be 'demi'.

As I sat down to sip cold beer and wipe the sweat from my forehead, a woman came through the door to join a couple of friends who were waiting for her.

"Brrr! It's freezing out there!"

She was wearing a full length woolen coat.

Detective Inspector Mick Bostock looks like a fairly typical New South Wales Cop - about seven foot tall with lugubrious, slightly baffled demeanour. Like all cops in this part of the world, he sported a black leather jacket. I jumped into the back of the squad car while Mick and another cop sat in front.

"You're gonna find a lot of media up there," he drawled. "They're kicking up a bit of a frenzy now they know you're coming".

We drove through the town, then carried on into the scrubby stuff beyond, down a rough country road that suddenly opened up into this hive of activity in the middle of nowhere. It reminded me of the bit in *'Apocalypse Now!'* when the guys in the gunboat arrive at a big US Army base in the Vietnamese jungle – but without those chicks in bikinis jumping out the helicopter. There were minibuses and four-wheel drives, squad cars and tents and a huddle of guys with cameras and microphone booms and pretty blondes cuddling clipboards. I was deposited on my own in a refreshments marquee while the cops sorted out what to do with me. I filched an orange for my pocket and munched on a ham sandwich while I waited. There were people outside, silently straining to get a glimpse of me through the gap in the flap of the marquee. Was Backpacker Dad quietly blubbing or praying or pummeling the ground with his fists in despair? Disappointingly - no. He was munching a ham sandwich.

After about ten minutes of this faintly disconcerting dumb-show, Mick came back with Sergeant Ian Collis. He was the officer in charge of the search. I was also introduced to a Police Media Liaison Officer whose name I did not catch. I was to see a lot of these guys over the next few days. Ian looked vaguely familiar. He explained that they were based here because it was the nearest part of the main plateau to the place where Jamie was thought to have been heading. For the first time, I heard the siren-call name of 'Mount Solitary'. There were about sixty guys searching down in the valley as we spoke and they were dropping people in by chopper to the most inaccessible bits. The trouble was that they couldn't be sure where Jamie had gone because he couldn't be bothered to write in the Bushwalk Register when he left the YHA. He had discussed going to Mount Solitary with some of the guys he met at the YHA, but it was all a bit vague and he might have changed his plans. I asked about joining the search. He said they were okay for volunteers. There was nothing to stop me bushwalking round the place by myself, but take a locator beacon with me. Ian was sure that Jamie wasn't wandering down any of the proper paths as hundreds of walkers used these every day and he would have met someone. They also had guys on trail bikes riding up and down. In other words, my own prospects of finding him were nil. I mentioned that he had taken a space blanket with him when he left Britain. As we talked, I realised why Ian looked so familiar. I was talking to Bing Crosby.

The Media Liaison guy showed me a screenshot of Jamie leaving the hostel on Friday the third. He was dressed in black jogging bottoms, dark blue jacket and strapped to a dark red knapsack. He might have been stepping out for a night exercise on Salisbury Plain. All he needed was a smudge of camouflage paint. I signed a bit of paper authorising release of this picture to the press. The guy asked if I was happy to talk to the media. I hadn't expected to be in demand like this, so I hadn't thought about what to say. He said it would help to publicise the search, maybe jog the mind of anyone who out there with useful information.

"Okay," I said.

I stood on the grass outside, in front of that gaggle of cameramen and clipboard carriers and sound recordists and told them not to worry about Jamie dying of exposure. "The cold won't kill him!"

"Aren't you cold?" said one of the blondes.

"No," I said. Why should I be on a warm day like this? They all had their coats on.

I told them I was born in Australia, but had been brought up in the UK since I was little.

"So you're an Aussie!"

"Nah, I'm as English as an *Oxo* cube!"

"What?" Some of them laughed.

"Don't you have them in Australia? Little silver stock cubes?"

The pursed lips, po-faced concern they had been putting on for my presumed benefit evaporated. This was not what they had been expecting. The missing boy's father was not a shambling, distraught, weeping wreck of a man. He was a bit of an end-of-pier comedian. It was my first step on the slippery slope of celebrity (from whence I slid to a distraught, shambling wreck of a man).

The media guy told me that Channel Nine was offering a chopper ride over the valley to search for my son. Wow! They would get the right to talk to me on film and I would get a chance to look for Jamie. Of course, it would be brilliant for them as well as me, especially if they got to film my face just as we spot the kid waving up at us from a rocky outcrop. So far as I was concerned, they could have anything they wanted out of me if it helped get Jamie back.

When everything was ready, I was escorted over to the helipad by Ian Collis. We strode across the tussocky grass, followed by cameramen stumbling as they struggled to focus on my face rather than their own feet. I asked Ian "Has anyone ever mentioned that you're a dead ringer for Bing Crosby?"

He looked nervous and ignored the question. I was suddenly very aware of the circle of microphones thrust out to catch my every utterance. I could read the next day's headline etched in Ian's face.

"Distraught Dad flies across world to discuss Bing Crosby look-alike shock with Search Supremo!"

I had a lot to learn about when to keep my mouth shut.

I was feeling pretty euphoric. I had made it to the place where my son was missing. After being sat helpless in a bedroom in Watford with a missing son and nothing to do but google 'Blue Mountains', here I was in those very same mountains and all set to go find him. I was pleased to see that the search was being conducted so intensively. I thought Jamie was still alive out there and so, apparently, did the police. Everyone was pretty upbeat about the kid's chances, especially now that last night's rainy weather had cleared and the choppers were able to operate. It was obvious to me now that he was missing rather than murdered and that, in itself, was a great weight off my mind. The encounter with the press pack had brought on a bit of an adrenalin rush and now I was going out to look for him in a chopper.

The ride in the Channel Nine helicopter soon brought me crashing back to earth - figuratively speaking. We took off and flew low over the same kind of scrub I'd seen on my drive in the squad car then, without warning, the ground plunged hundreds of feet beneath us and we were looking at billions of trees undulating away to the end of the earth. We had crossed over the edge of a cliff. Up until this moment, I hadn't understood the way the landscape worked round here. It had all been hidden until that moment of revelation. We followed the line of a creek towards Mount Solitary. If Jamie had stood in the stream we would have spotted him easily. If he had gone just thirty feet either side he would have been lost in the trees. The trees seemed to go on south forever, though bounded on the north and east side by the Kedumba Walls. I stared out the window, eager for anything that looked out of place in this ocean of green and grey trees and honey-coloured rock. All the time I was fielding questions from the blonde, who is probably ever so famous in Oz, though her name is forgotten to me. They all looked the same. We hovered over Mount Solitary. Incredibly, there were a couple of people lounging on the rocks on top. I was amazed how anyone could find their way through all those miles of forest to get there. The helicopter pilot showed the path that led back to Katoomba. It was only when we were right over the track that it was distinguishable from the forest on either side. There was a guy in a shiny yellow jacket walking up to the mountain. He was the only one of Ian's sixty searchers we spotted. We were on the lookout for a kid in black, dark blue and burgundy. It was the cliffs that really brought home to me what my son was up against. We slowly orbited the Mount Solitary Plateau, maybe looking for a burgundy bag hanging on a branch or spatter of blood on a rock. I could see how easy it would be to come crashing through the trees in gathering darkness and maybe not see the edge till it was too late to stop. I'd never seen inland cliffs like it - except in a film based on Arthur Conan Doyle's 'Lost World' and those cliffs had pterodactyls flapping over them. It seemed, in my anguish, to be a terrifying and primordial place to be lost or stuck somewhere with a broken leg, or even with brain cells spattered across twenty yards of bloody sandstone, soon to be flushed away by last night's rain.

"What's happened to you, Jamie? Where are you?"

The trees stayed mute.

"We'll take a spin round Narrow Neck," said the pilot. He pointed out a rocky outcrop that rose from the forest in between. "That's 'Ruined Castle' over there".

More dizzy cliffs and then we were staring down at the ribbon of road across the incredibly narrow isthmus of Narrow Neck with a sheer drop down on either side.

"Do people actually drive across?" I gasped.

"There's a barrier across the road to stop public access, but police and the ranger service use it. There's a fire watch lookout on the plateau".

They were scaring me silly and they knew it.

Months later, when I recall that day, I realise that Channel Nine lost a trick when they took me to all the wrong places to look for Jamie. This was their land and they were keen to show it off to the pasty-faced Pom flown in from the Home Counties. The scenery was fantastic, mind blowing, but in my particular circumstances, it made my blood run cold. When my niece came over from Australia, I didn't seek to impress her with her in the dreary clay prairies of Hertfordshire. I took her to see the ancient White Horse of Uffington and we climbed up to the tower on Glastonbury Tor. She would never see anything like these places back home Down Under. It was the same for the crew in the chopper. They treated me to a high altitude, high speed tour of the glories of the Jamison Valley. A few miles south of Narrow Neck the landscape is less spectacular. The drops are more survivable and the jagged nature of the tumbled rocks is softened by trees that snake up between them. From where we were it seemed an undulating, tree-covered landscape, almost featureless as it spun away into the distant haze, broken only by creeks as commonplace as the one we'd followed from the search base. This was a shame for me, for Jamie and for Channel Nine. If they had swung the chopper out over this, less spectacular, bit of the terrain, maybe we might have spotted someone down there, desperately waving a grubby, pale blue shirt. And they would have got to film the biggest and most saleable scoop that ever hit their TV station. It was a shame it didn't happen like that. I remain grateful for the flight. Even if my son were not lost, I would happily have paid a fortune for the experience.

We headed back to base camp and the flight ended where it had begun, but my mood had darkened. The chopper ride had offered me the best chance of personally finding Jamie and now it was over and he was still out there, maybe lost, maybe injured, maybe dead. The cliffs gave me a lot to think about. They were tall enough to dwarf a skyscraper. If my boy had fallen off, then he was definitely dead. I still hung on to the hope he might be injured and that was why he couldn't walk out, but the hope that he was simply lost and wandering in circles had taken a knock when I saw how much of a search was going on. He had had plenty of time to walk out, if he was able to walk at all. I was starting to wonder whether my earlier optimism might have been, well... over-optimistic.

The next treat was being driven around in a jeep by a lady Park Ranger. Ian had been contacted by the British High Commission and they had arranged accommodation for me. Lois would show me the way to get down to the Ruined Castle walking track and then she'd take me to the hotel. We got on okay. As we bucked down a potholed dirt track leading to the top of The Golden Stairs, I told her about the time I got stuck on a farm track in Dorset. I'd had the brilliant idea of driving up this track so that we could look down on the Cerne Abbas Giant from the top of a neighbouring hill. Why park up with everyone else in the car park down below and dodge crowds and picnic tables to stand in awe of the most brilliant chalk figure in England - a club-wielding, goggle eyed curmudgeon with thirty foot of upstart phallus? How this generously endowed brute managed to evade desecration or emasculation by Puritan or Victorian iconoclasts is a mystery to be pondered upon. Even in my childhood, nothing so ribald would ever have been knowingly permitted to sully my innocence. Lois had never heard of the Giant so I said I'd send her a post card when I got back home. I had checked out the map and thought my idea of looking down from above was 'do-able'. It just happened to be the hottest day in England since records began, August 10th, 2003. The tractorial ruts in the baked mud path got deeper and deeper until the car's sump and floor pan grounded on the ridge in between. The wheels were turning but the car wasn't going anywhere. I struggled manfully in the blistering heat for a couple of hours, hacking at rock hard soil with a scissor jack and a plastic sea-side spade. Jean and the kids sat down in the shade of a hedge while I battled on, horseflies biting flesh and bluebottles sucking up sweat. I snatched our only bottle of water from the cracked lips of the children to sustain daddy's strength to carry on digging. In the end I gave up and called the RAC. It might have been a very Australian family tragedy played out on some lonely track across the Nullarbor Plain, but this was Dorset so what panned out was a very English family farce. As the breakdown truck lifted up the front of the car, a two litre bottle of lemonade rolled out from under my seat.

After the road to the steps, Lois drove me to Echo Point, a viewpoint for those spectacular stacks of sandstone known as 'The Three Sisters'.

I recognised these Sisters from a calendar that Jeff had brought over the previous year. As I strolled through the crowd of tourists, camera crews silently circled me in small stealthy war bands, like Apache Indians. The public who were here to see 'The Sisters' must have wondered who I was, this Falstaffian buffoon shadowed by paparazzi, like he was some kinda pop star or something.

The press attention was becoming annoying. How was I supposed to go about my business with this kind of fuss buzzing around me? I asked Lois to pick up my bags from the van while I booked into the hotel. I didn't want the press to get to know my vehicle. I gave her the key, then she dropped me at *The Carrington*, the swankiest hotel in Katoomba.

The Carrington is a luxurious and expensive five star hotel. It's not the sort of place I would stay, even if someone else was paying and I wasn't sure whether I was the one paying. I felt out of place from the moment I walked up the steps. I gave my name to the concierge but he had no record of a booking. I explained that I'd been sent there by the British High Commission. I was father of the lad who was lost in the bush and I was subject to intense and unwelcome media attention. He led me to a bar and suggested I get myself a cup of coffee while he looked for the manager. I sat down to drink the most expensive cup of tea that I have ever imbibed. After a few minutes, the man was back with his boss. There had been a mistake.

They had no vacancy. My room was at another hotel at the other end of Katoomba - *The Palais Royal*.

When Lois arrived, hauling my bags, I told her I wasn't staying. We jumped back in the jeep. *The Palais Royal* turned out to be located right next to the place where I had parked the van. It was opposite the YHA. Despite the high-faluting name of the place, *The Palais Royal* turned out to be a comfortable, considerate and unpretentious place to stay. I did end up with a bill to pay, but it was not too bad and they let my brother share the room for free. It was perfectly located for cop shop and the YHA; a lot less stuffy than *The Carrington*. I had had a lucky escape. I thought the High Commission had been pretty high-handed in booking accommodation for me in the first place. I hadn't asked them to do it. What did they know about my budget? How did they know I hadn't brought a tent along with me?

Chapter Six

The Bush

The earliest known written record which makes use, in English, of the word 'bush' is to be found in a charter of the Abbey of Peterborough, where it forms part of the place name 'Withinbuscmere' - the willow bush pond. This is dated sometime before 1022 - contemporary with King Canute. The word was, and still is, a familiar one. Many an English alehouse has gone by the name of 'The Holly Bush' or 'The Ivy Bush'. Indeed, in former times, a hank of ivy hung above the door was recognised as the generic sign for a tavern - ivy being considered sacred to Bacchus, Roman god of wine. Rosalind refers to this convention in Shakespeare's 'As You Like It': *"For if it be true that a good wine needs no bush..."* - no doubt to the bewilderment of nine tenths of the modern audience who enjoy wine, good or bad, without benefit of bush.

The word is found in a number of 'well-known sayings' - 'A bird in the hand is worth two in the bush' and 'Let's not beat around the bush!'. The simile 'Like an owl in an ivy bush' is less familiar. It refers to a fixed and bewildered stare. There are fourteen references to 'bush' in the King James Bible, mostly with reference to God's manifestation before Moses in the form of a bush that burned without itself being consumed.

This bush became a means of referring to God, whilst avoiding the holy name.

"For the good will of him who lived in the bush, let the blessing come on the head of Joseph," Deuteronomy, 33:16.

In these contexts, the word 'bush' denotes some kind of shrub or woody plant - of modest stature in comparison to a tree. Similar and related words occur in many other Indo-European languages - Danish 'busk', Old French 'busche (= firewood) and modern German, 'busch'. According to the *Middle English Dictionary*, compiled at the University of Michigan (Lewis, Kuhn and Kurath), the English word is derived from the Latin form 'bosca', meaning firewood. As the Germanic and Scandinavian forms are closer in form and meaning to the English word, I find their conclusion surprising.

The sense of the word 'bush' or, more accurately, 'the bush' to describe an area of uncultivated and sparsely populated country was first recorded in American English in 1657. It is thought that this was in imitation of Dutch usage. At that time, what is now the US state of New York constituted the Dutch colony of New Amsterdam. The Dutch were also active on the southern tip of the African Continent and it was here that this bush, or bosch, first began to branch out into such familiar combinations as bushbuck (bosch-bok) and bushman (bosjesman - first recorded 1785).

The word is no longer much used in North America, where hikers walk 'the wilderness' or go 'up country'. Nor can one sensibly 'go bush' in Great Britain. There are heaths and moors and highlands to be found, but no truly equivalent phrase to describe all these tracts of uncultivated country. The nearest equivalent is a lovely archaism familiar to admirers of Robin Hood - the greenwood.

So it is only in the Southern Hemisphere and in Australia in particular, that 'the bush' has come to loom so large in the consciousness of a nation. The limits of its application are somewhat labile. My Chambers Twentieth Century Dictionary (1971) offers the definition "Wild uncultivated country (even though treeless)". Other authorities specifically exclude those areas of

Australia so arid that progress is unimpeded by the local flora. The traveller is then deemed to have gone beyond 'the bush' and entered another iconic Australian landscape - 'The Outback' or 'Back-Of-Beyond'.

In its new home beneath The Southern Cross, 'the bush' has blossomed into literally scores of new combinations - bush tucker, bushwalker, bush telegraph, bushranger etc. The word can function as noun, verb or adjective. To 'go bush' is to live outside the actual and metaphorical limits of society. "To get 'bushed' is to become lost in the gum forests". (H. M. Vaughan, An Australian Wonder, 1914). The earliest recorded reference to 'the bush' in an Australian context is found in the journal of Lieutenant Ralph Clark of the Marines, dated 1790. This is only a couple of years after the arrival of the first fleet. His laconic report seems to reverberate down the years as leitmotif for that long uncomprehending encounter between colonist and colonised *"They had run into the bush on there (sic) seeing the boat pulling towards them"*. In 1803, a dourly humorous piece in the Sydney Gazette recommended *'parts of the bush'* as a dance academy *'with the assistance of the accomplished kangaroo'*.

J. D. Lang's 'Historical and Statistical Account of New South Wales' (1834) relates that *"The word 'bush' which sometimes signifies the country in general, but more properly the uncleared part of it, is mainly the Dutch word 'bosch', signifying wood as fuel"*. All citations are from The Oxford University *'Dictionary of Australian English'*.

Jamie was to be apostrophised as 'The Boy in the Bush'. For eleven nights he was 'Lost in the Bush'. He was described at various times as 'an experienced bushwalker' and 'an inexperienced bushwalker'.

There is a third usage of the term 'bush', largely unrelated, except in imagination or metaphor, to that warm, dank and musky place where I thrashed about for my son's sake. In 1966, Topic Records released a collection of English folk songs, sung by various artists, under the general title of one of its more memorable tracks. This album was subtitled *'Traditional Songs of Love and Lust'*. Nor did A.L.Lloyd's sleeve notes beat about the bush:

"In poetry, as in dream, the bird may be a mild symbol of the penis, as the rose, rosebush or bush is the vulva". There were nineteen tracks in all, with such titles as *'The Old Bachelor'*, *'The Bonny Black Hare'* and *'The Cock'*. The song promoted to stand title for the collection as a whole was sung by Frankie Armstrong. It was called *'The Bird in the Bush'*.

Similar songs, sometimes with dissimilar titles, were recorded by other notable interpreters of English Folk Music - such as Shirley Collins, Anne Briggs, Steeleye Span (*Drink down the Moon*) and Norma Watson (*Three Pretty Maidens*). The scarcely concealed erotic imagery of the lyrics seems to have embarrassed those middle class Victorian 'collectors' who were the first to take an educated interest in traditional English folksong. The song was originally published in a heavily bowdlerised form. The following, uncensored, lyrics of the Frankie Armstrong version give something of the flavour:

"So away to the greenwoods went they,
And he tapped at the bush and the bird it did fly in,
Just a little above her lily white knee.

Here's a health to the bird in the bush,
And we'll drink down the moon and we'll drink up the sun,
Let the neighbours say little or much".

So far as the Blue Mountains is concerned 'the bush' consists of a seemingly endless vista of eucalyptus trees. You stand on the edge of the cliff that forms the southern boundary of the town of Katoomba and, as Charles Darwin pointed out, it is like staring down at the ocean from high coastal cliffs. There is nothing in the British landscape to compare with these inland cliffs, plunging vertically down into that sea of blue-green leaves below. Nothing to compare with mile upon mile of tree canopy laid out to the utmost horizon and beyond. Down there 'in the valley' there appears to be no sign of human intervention. Look back at Katoomba and there are street lamps and paths and 'Scenic World', places to eat, rest and be cheerful. Turn to face the valley and you see what Darwin saw when he came this way in 1836. Give or take the odd landslide, you see what the dreamtimers saw before white men came meddling. They left traces of their time on Kings Tableland in the form of rocks scarred by their axe sharpening. You see what the great Australian mega-fauna saw before black men and dingoes ran giant kangaroos to extinction, 40,000 years ago. There's a lot of bush out there, but you don't actually need a lot of bush to get lost. In 1867 the bodies of three children were found in and around a hollow tree, near Daylsford, Victoria, about two hundred yards from a road in daily use. The bones were brought in by the dog of a man who lived close by. These babes had been missing for over two months.

It must be said that, from the heights, this view is deceptive. There are man-made paths down there, even vehicular access for those who maintain power lines and manage the waters. There are old mine workings and remains of coalminers' cottages mouldering beneath the trees and leaf litter. But nothing of this can be seen from the cliff top. The picture comprises one vast, impenetrable forest, like something from medieval legend. There is even a 'Ruined Castle' thrusting up halfway between the tip of Narrow Neck and that brooding cliff-girt, tree-clad plateau of Mount Solitary, breaching like an island from the blue eucalyptine sea.

'Mount Solitary'. Now, if ever was coined a name to gather dauntless souls to destruction, then whoever christened this rock must surely take that biscuit. The walk from the Golden Stairs to Mount Solitary is earmarked 'for serious walkers only' on the rudimentary map issued by the Blue Mountain YHA. This was, in fact, my son's only guide to the walk he set upon on that fateful third of July. It is just possible to get there and back in a day, much easier to do so in summer when the sun doesn't go down before five o'clock. For serious walkers who are prepared to camp out overnight there is little problem. It is possible to descend into the valley by the Golden Stairs, take the level track to the base of 'Ruined Castle', scramble up the slope of broken rocks and fallen trees to the admire the view from the top of the castle, carry on to rejoin the old colliery railway path, then on to Mount Solitary itself. Once the walker has made it up to the mountaintop, a path traverses the length of that pixie-boot shaped plateau, then drops back down to the valley floor at its gusset end. After many weary miles, the prescribed bushwalk fetches up at the base of cliffs by Kings Tableland. A steep and winding path leads our serious walker back into the comforting ambience of driveways, lawns and motor cars.

When men from the shires of England first arrived in this Great Southern Continent, they found much that was not right about the landscape, the animal life and the vegetation. They set about replacing the unfamiliar with reminders of the land they had left behind - rabbits and roses, oak trees and apple orchards. The native trees of Australia seemed particularly recalcitrant. They remained defiantly leaf-lacking in comparison with the beech trees, oaks and elms of the old country. In a land where shade was so much in demand, standing timber sulkily begrudged to offer more than a kind of dappled semi-interposition between high burning sun and sun-blasted sojourner below. Their colour was all wrong too. In England, trees are green. A rich, dark emerald green - till summer's lease hath gone and those green, green leaves turn red and gold and fly off in the gales of November. The leaves of these ubiquitous eucalypts are not green, nor are they blue or even grey but some insipid in-between shade, like an overwashed, sun-bleached pair of overalls. The leaves look their best in the Southern Winter. In summer the tree simply seems to invite combustion. Not only are the leaves desiccated, drooping or actually dropping off but they exude some kind of highly combustible vapour which hangs about them like a blue haze. Of course, modern botanists have a much greater understanding of why the eucalyptus does what it does and thrives while doing it. Trees that spread their leaves to catch every photon of light beaming down from the cloudy skies of England do so because they need to make the most of a scanty and intermittent energy source. God did not so design them with a view to provide shade for man and his beasts. That same eagerness for Britannia's begrudgingly offered sunbeams also explains why the leaves of north European trees are abundantly supplied with the green photosensitive pigment, chlorophyll. Australian skies supply more than enough energy for growth and reproduction. The problem is to limit absorption of sunlight to protect the plant from desiccation and overheating, hence the pale green-grey foliage, fewer leaves and waxy exudations to keep moisture from evaporating away. Despite being seemingly deficient in the means to convert sunlight into new wood, gum trees grow so fast that they can provide sustainable green fuel for wood-fired power stations. Their rapid growth keeps pace with the ever consuming furnace. Eucalyptus trees are now widely planted for paper pulp, timber and fuel. Their essential oils sooth throats and dissolve snot.

There are something like eight hundred different species of Eucalyptus, including the related genera of Corymbia and Angophora. Most are found in the continent of Australia, others occur in New Guinea and other islands of Indonesia. The Blue Mountains are home to about a hundred species. Some of the trees are stunning specimens with ghost white trunks soaring high into the canopy. Others have bark that hangs in tatters or strips of cordage. Yet more are scrubby, bush-like forms that hinder progress and knock your hat off as you struggle to push on through.

The first Europeans to encounter trees that would one day be classified as Eucalypts were spice-seeking Dutchmen in what is now the Indonesian Archipelago. The Dutch were also the first Europeans to blunder against the coast of Australia. They were not impressed. Nor was William Dampier. Dampier was the first Englishman to look an Aussie in the face and record the experience. Dampier fetched up on Australia's northern shore in 1688 and went on to describe the fly tormented locals he found there as 'the miserablest People in the world'.

It was a different story when James Cook gazed upon the continent's much balmier south-eastern coast in the company of botanist, Sir Joseph

Banks. It was the British who were first to appreciate that this eucalyptine Eden might be profitably cleared to make way for wheat fields and cattle pastures - that these fine trees were better employed as fence posts or clapboard for farmers than perches for parrots or leaning posts for idle indigenes. The practical application of this insight was realised through the sweat of the old country's criminal classes. Having stumbled upon a benign formula for the sustenance of a self-supporting colony in this far-off land, it became settled policy of successive Hanoverian governments that no Frenchman should obtain foothold in the land of the unfree. Australia - dismissed by the Dutch, colonised by Britannia - was to remain forever a Frog-free zone. It therefore comes as a shock to learn that neither Sir Joseph Banks nor Mijnheer Herman Boerhaave were first to describe, classify and nominate the genus *Eucalyptus,* but Monsieur Charles Louis L'Heritier de Brutelle, Superintendent of Parisian Waters and Forests. The name means 'well-covered', with reference to the form of the buds. Of course, these same species had already been given other names by people who had walked beneath them for 50,000 years before Captain Cook waded dauntlessly ashore.

There are no dangerous animals in the Jamison Valley, apart from snakes which sleep out the chilly weather. There are wombats, sugar gliders and wallabies, as well as feral pigs and horses. The dense vegetation means that these creatures are seldom seen, though their droppings and their paths through the undergrowth may be observed by those with the wit to notice them. There is plenty of birdlife to see and hear. Lyrebirds, bush turkeys and parrots are locally abundant. Small, sparrow-sized birds peck at crumbs dropped from bushwalker lunch packs. At times, depending on the sunshine and the direction of slope, the forest resounds to the squawk of parrots or the territorial coos of the lyrebirds. At other times, the path is dark, dank and silent.

In winter, the creeks flow freely with water cascading down from the inhabited plateau in a garland of waterfalls - Katoomba Falls, Leura Cascades, Gordon Falls and The Bridal Veil. In high summer these streams can fail. Although the valley is well watered in winter, it is not always easy to get down to the stream. The fast flowing waters cut into the sandstone, forming steep, cliff lined gorges. The horizontal bedding plane of the layers of sandstone, with softer beds of shale, encourages water to undercut the base of the cliff, eventually causing a section to shear off and tumble down into the stream below. Flash floods carry away the detritus leaving a sheer cliff-face soaring above the foaming waters. Over many millennia, running water, aided by frost and bush-fire and the rummage of lyrebirds, has washed away billions of tons of rock from the region to create the awesome, amphitheatre-like valley that today stretches so dizzyingly away from the Leura-Katoomba Plateau to the distant horizon.

Two hundred and fifty million years ago most of eastern New South Wales was beneath a shallow sea off the shore of the huge continental landmass of Pangaea. What is now the east coast of Australia was then the south coast. The continental plate, along with its submarine continental shelf, has since drifted anticlockwise. Rivers flowing into this sea from the 'north' dumped layers of sandy sediments upon the ocean floor. A few million years later the area became a shallow, fresh water swamp. As conditions did not favour decay, the fallen vegetation became compacted into a dense mass of carbon rich biomass. The region became inundated by the sea once more and layer upon layer of sand piled upon those seams of swamp flora, crushing and transforming the stuff from peat, to lignite, to coal. At times the sands were replaced by freshwater mud which now outcrops as layers of shale, but it was sandstone that came to dominate the local geology. About two hundred million years ago, during the early Jurassic period, isolated volcanoes burst through the layers of sandy sediment. More recently, about twenty million years ago, a huge basaltic lava flow covered most of the Blue Mountain region. Finally, the area was uplifted, causing fast flowing rivers and streams to cut down into the horizontal layers of rock, washing away immense volumes of sandstone, shale and basalt, to create the deeply incised landscape of today. The lava flow that once blanketed the thick layers of sandstone is now almost entirely eroded away, except for isolated caps on Mount Tomah, Mount Banks and Mount Irvine. I saw no igneous rocks in the search for my son. I saw a fair bit of coal, but it was those massive sandstone cliffs which dominated the view above the trees, sheer crags of rock plunging vertically down through layer after layer of yellow, brown and orange to the talus slope at base of the cliff. In places, where some especially tough stratum resists gravity and the elements better than the layers above, a narrow shelf will linger halfway up a cliff. There may perhaps be room enough for a strip of eucalyptus shrubs and trees to take root, until the next landslide shrugs them off from their place in the sun. Until that day only the odd flying bird would ever touch them. Unless some unfortunate young man comes screaming down from above, to wedge his broken body out of sight between trees and cliff and hang there, undiscovered, till doomsday.

Chapter Seven

The Search

I laid my things out in the hotel room and phoned up Jean. I told her about my adventure with the helicopter and how seriously they were conducting the search. I got a call from Maureen in Perth to say Jeff was on the train and he should arrive in Katoomba around six o'clock. She would let him know where I was staying. My phone battery was almost out of juice and my domestic charger wouldn't fit the Australian sockets. I went out to the van to plug my in-car charger into the socket on the dashboard. The power only flowed when key was in the ignition. I got so frustrated by this glitch, that I sat there fuming for a few minutes, then decided to drive down to the station to wait for Jeff. That way I'd charge up my phone and save my brother a walk at the same time. It was dark by this time, but I caught sight of him in the headlamps and executed a tyre-shredding U-turn at the main crossroads of Katoomba. We were only about seventy yards away from the hotel entrance. There was a different receptionist on duty now, so I explained about Jeff being my brother and how he would be staying in my room by arrangement with Albert. I always worry about sharing accommodation with Jeff. I like to make it clear that he is not my gay partner and we will be requiring separate beds.

The next day, Albert lent me an adapter so I could charge up my phone. In a pattern that was to become familiar, this act of kindness went on to have fateful consequences. I handed back the adapter when I left the hotel. If I had not got one from Albert, I would have bought my own adapter and I would have been able to charge up my phone batteries in Jamie's hospital, with better consequences than those that transpired.

It was great to see Jeff again, even though it was only the previous October that he had stayed with me in Watford. We had gone off on a road trip to North Wales to climb a mountain together. Yr Eifl is a lovely mountain to scramble up, with a prehistoric 'Troy Town' on the summit. We had a look at the castles at Harlech and Caernarvon and enjoyed some *craic* with locals at a pub in Caernarvon, watching Spurs draw four-all with Arsenal on the pub TV. We even got given free Smirnoff bobble-hats from behind the bar. When we stepped out into the night outside, it was as if an icicle had been rammed down my throat. It was as cold as I've ever known it. Even I shuddered in my fleecy jacket. If Aussies think they're cold in the Blue Mountains, they should sample that October breeze off the Menai Strait.

Jeff had been disconcerted by an incident that happened on the train up from Sydney. The guy sitting beside him hadn't said a word but, as he got up to go, he leaned over to Jeff and pointed out a line written in the book he had been reading.

"When you're in Hell, keep going".

It was one of those inexplicable happenings that dogged our time in New South Wales. It was as though God was playing around with us. I know my brother too well to think he would make up anything like that.

Jeff had brought over some of the stuff Jamie had left behind in Perth, including his Duke of Edinburgh Silver Wallet stuffed with currency. Our mum had also wired some cash over to Jeff and he handed it to me. We did not spend Jamie's money.

I described my day and described what I'd seen from the chopper ride. I said the police were hopeful that Jamie was still alive; especially when I told them he had a space blanket.

"Actually, he left that at my place." interjected Jeff.

I raised two fists and my face to the ceiling and released a silent scream. We watched the news on the telly, footage of me talking about Jamie never getting cold, footage of me in the chopper, willing him to show himself as I gaze intently down at the sea of trees, wide-eyed with apprehension as I survey those precipitous cliffs.

Then we opted to wander down the high street of Katoomba to find somewhere to eat. The Antipodal air had rekindled my appetite. We eventually stopped at the same place where I had sipped my beer several hours before. They had a copy of *'The Telegraph'* with Jamie on the cover. I ordered the steak pie and chips and sat back to drink my beer. The waitress returned with the disappointing news that there was no pie tonight and could I please order something else.

Karl Marx reckoned that history comes round twice - initially as tragedy, the second time as farce. Sometimes the tragedy and the farce seem to run contemporaneously alongside one another, a kind of parallel trajectory of fate. The very serious, very worrying search for my lost son was mirrored almost move for move by my simultaneous search for the Great Australian Meat Pie. I eventually found that pastry topped Holy Grail of a pie, a whole pie shop full of them in fact, as I stumbled grief-stricken back to Sidney Airport after I'd dropped off the van. Two hours later I got my son back. There was once a time when Australian Cuisine was so dismally disparaged, even by its own children, that 'pie and chips' became a metonymic term of abuse, shorthand for the whole gamut of Anglo-Antipodean plain cooking from suet dumplings to apple crumble. A foodie reaction set in and nowadays it may be easier to dine on sweet potato gnocchi than tuck in to a steak and kidney pie with chips and gravy anywhere beneath the Southern Cross. For some strange reason they still write it on the menu, maybe some kind of retro kitsch, recalling those bad old days of the forties and fifties. I ordered meat pie on three separate occasions in three different places and each time it was unavailable. "We only put it on the menu to lend a note of cod authenticity to the proceedings. We never expected anyone to actually order and eat the stuff!" They didn't say that last bit. I also apologise unreservedly to the teenage girl behind the servery at Scenic World for making such a scene about this - pun unintended. I had spent a long day searching for my son. I was tired. I was hungry.

Back on that first night in Katoomba, I re-perused the menu and plumped for the barramundi. I had never tasted this iconic Australian fish dish before. Jeff reckons they sometimes serve up hake if they think you won't be able to tell the difference. I wouldn't. The fish was dished up with some pan fried vegetables that tasted only of the oil in which they were fried. I did not think much of the fish either. In the morning I had the squits. The redeeming feature of this misadventure was that I was able to make light of the griping in my guts through reference to a parody of Michael Jackson, who happened to have been found dead the previous month.

"Don't blame it on the sunshine, don't blame it on the moonlight, don't blame it on the good times. Blame it on the barramundi".

It was great to have my big brother around. He knew this kind of flippancy did not mean I wasn't worried about my son.

The next day we headed up to the base camp. I had to get directions from the police station as I couldn't remember how I'd got there yesterday. Still no news of Jamie. Ian Collis gave Jeff a beacon so we couldn't get lost and arranged for a Park Ranger to show us the way to the castle. We followed the ranger's jeep down the track to the Golden Stairs and parked nearby. There were a few search guys hanging about. I shook their hands and told them I was grateful for what they were doing. Then it was a scramble down the steps to join the old mine railway track to Ruined Castle. These steps are known as 'The Golden Stairs' because miners would sing a hymn about *'Going up the Golden Stairs'* while they were going up them. So, nothing to do with all this golden coloured sandstone then? It's a long and difficult descent on a steep track with steel barriers and wire rope to stop you falling off in some places. This is one of a handful of places where it is possible to get down from the inhabited plateau to enter the uninhabited forest below the cliffs.

When we got to the bottom of the cliffs we emerged onto a level path that ran parallel to the cliff line. It was constructed as a horse-drawn tramway for hauling shale and coal from Ruined Castle back to Katoomba. It was easy walking and we were able to talk over the search with Arthur as we made our way to the castle. I asked whether they were using infrared detectors on choppers during the night. Arthur said they were but it was difficult to see through the tree cover. There were some warm animals moving around at night - bush turkeys, wallabies, wild horses and hogs. I was surprised to hear about the horses and hogs. We saw very little wildlife, though the bush was noisy with birdcalls. Every so often I would shout Jamie's name. There were little red ribbons tied to some of the tree branches. Arthur said these were left by the search parties to show that the area had been thoroughly searched. I was wasting my breath. He showed us the footings of the old coalminers' cottages and campsites, places where they had sat and drank and swapped yarns until early in the twentieth century. We arrived at the foot of the path that deviated up to 'Ruined Castle' at about four in the afternoon. On Arthur's advice, we did not go up. It would be dark by six and unwise to tackle The Golden Stairs in poor light. The track was on the shady side of the cliff as the sun set in the west. We headed back. The Golden Stairs were such an effort to ascend that I needed to stop and rest about six times before I got to the top. Arthur had told us about a historic landslide that had destroyed part of the level path between the Scenic Railway and The Golden Stairs, obliterating about half a mile of the horse-drawn railway track. Because that level and obvious path had been buried under fallen rock, hikers sometimes lost their way in traversing the talus from the landslide to link up the surviving stretches of track. We did not know what route Jamie had used to come down into the valley. If he had made use of the Scenic Railway or The Giant's Causeway, he would have passed that way. The landslide would provide our focus for the following day.

We drove back to Katoomba for fish and chips. It was Saturday night. We finished up drinking at Gearin's Hotel.

On Sunday Morning, I found an Internet cafe and typed out a letter of appreciation for the men and women who were participating in the search. Many of them were volunteer fire-fighters. I wrote out some thoughts about Jamie and why he was so special that they had to keep looking for him so long as any hope remained. It was the least I could do for them. The least I could do for Jamie. Since the day I wrote that eulogy to a lost son, my son has come back and things haven't worked out as well between us as they should have done. I would still not alter a syllable of what I wrote. It is as true today as it was then. Jamie is a special boy.

The hotel ran off sixty copies, I signed each one and drove down to the base. I asked if they could try to give every volunteer a copy.

Then I drove back to the hotel and parked the van. We walked to Scenic World to take a ride down into the valley. Jamie had walked along the same streets nine days earlier. There were four bronze statues outside the entrance to this tourist attraction - three stark naked aboriginal maidens and a wizened, bollock-naked, old man. These bronzes recall a native Australian legend about the old man turning his daughters to stone to protect them from a bunyip, or evil spirit. Then he turned himself into a lyre-bird but somehow dropped the magic bone he needed to reverse the spell. Those three sisters still stand as picturesque stacks of rock while Old Man Lyre Bird still rummages through the leaf litter, eternally seeking the missing magic bone. I took a photo. Jeff and the maidens. Jeff took a photo. Rick poses with the old man and his bone. Please don't smile.

We had a choice between the world's steepest railway train or the cable car ride. On my map, it looked as though the cable car went further down and further along the path to Ruined Castle.

So we went down by cable. When we got to the bottom, we were in a fenced off area, walking on a boardwalk circuit which eventually brought us to the railway terminus. There were trees alongside, or actually imprisoned within, the boardwalk. These trees had been fitted with labels which described their names and information about their growth - as individual trees rather than as species. I remembered the Joni Mitchell line about putting all the trees in a tree museum *"and charge the people a dollar and a half just to see 'em"*. We paid a lot more than that. We had blundered by error into this blend of nature and artifice and were worn out by the time we finally found our way on to the 'Ruined Castle Track'.

About half a mile from our starting point, the broad and level track vanishes and it was necessary to pick our way across a confusion of massive boulders guided by a line of coloured stakes. As we struggled across the debris of this eighty year old landslide, we met up with a team of searchers who were checking the nooks and crannies between the boulders. I introduced myself as Jamie's dad and asked if I could take a photo for Jean back home. They were friendly and hard-working men. I felt humbled that they were doing so much for my son. The camera had flattened the batteries and I couldn't take the picture. One guy offered me batteries from his pocket, told me I could keep them. The camera still demanded more power before it was prepared to deploy. One of these magnificent blokes thanked me for the letter I had left at the search base. These volunteers were unselfish heroes in the way they quietly got on with their allotted tasks. When there were fictions published in the Australian press about me being greedy for money or media exposure, it broke my heart to think that men and women such as these would read those made up stories and probably wonder why they had bothered.

Jeff and I carried on to 'Ruined Castle' walking past the point where we had come down The Golden Stairs the day before. At the top of 'Ruined Castle', I climbed the jumble of eroded rocks that gives the place its name. The view was magnificent, with an amphitheatre of precipitous cliffs enclosing the undulating heart of the park. Mount Solitary lay about four or five miles further along the track. There was a sign saying, 'for serious walkers only'. My hat went spinning off in the breeze and I had to ask Jeff to collect it from where it fell.

The walk up had been a tough scramble, but nothing dangerous. You might twist your ankle, indeed Jeff did do just that two days later, but there was no way you could simply disappear off the face of the planet for such a long time. It just didn't seem right that Jamie could come to grief on the walk we had just completed. We had met families with toddlers on the path, wizened greybeards and women in their eighties. I elected to return to the main path by going straight down the short side of the long, caterpillar shaped elevation that we stood upon. I wanted to see how easy it was to move through the bush without a proper path.

I got to the bottom without incident. The hat got knocked off by a stray branch once or twice and vines did sometimes lasso my ankles, but there was nothing remotely dangerous or difficult about what I had done. Jamie had said he was making for 'Ruined Castle'. He had said he might go on to Mount Solitary. I thought Jamie would not have chosen to go further than the castle. In 2008, I had climbed up Yr Eifl with Jeff. Yr Eifl means 'the fork' in Welsh. The name refers to the three peaks separated by high saddle-shaped gullies. Through a happy but circumstantial assonance, their English name is 'The Rivals', as though the three peaks were actually vying for supremacy. I had first climbed this mountain with Jamie in 2001, when my son was getting on for twelve years old. He hadn't seemed to enjoy the slog and when I suggested we cross over the saddle to the highest peak of the three that make up Yr Eifl, he declined. He had done enough. It was raining and he already had enough sheep shit on his new trainers. I reasoned that he would behave the same way when he faced that sign about the walk to Solitary. He would not strive to do anything too physically demanding in these mountains. The 'Ruined Castle' bushwalk would be enough to be getting on with.

As there was nothing perilous between Katoomba and 'Ruined Castle', then perhaps the police had got it wrong. Perhaps he had gone somewhere else, somewhere where there was real danger and isolation. I had bought a guidebook to bushwalks in the Blue Mountains. Many of the walks featured waterfalls. I love waterfalls. On our last family holiday together we had stayed on the coast near Conwy. On the day after we arrived we walked up to Aber Falls to see one of the highest and most voluminous waterfalls in North Wales. I could see was a pattern to Jamie's holiday plans. The visits to Hanoi and Moscow to see the tombs of the dead dictators were echoes of our trip to see Karl Marx. He was intending to enjoy an eclipse of the sun taking place in Kathmandu, just like the eclipse we'd enjoyed together in Cornwall when he was nine. Maybe this pattern of doing things he'd done before with me was the clue to where he had gone missing. What was the first thing I would go see when sightseeing in the Blue Mountains? It was a waterfall. The police knew the geography. They knew what he had said to the people at the Youth Hostel, but they did not know my son as well as me. He may have intended to go to the 'Ruined Castle' on another day, but he had gone to see a waterfall on the Friday. This was why there was a message for me stored on his phone, about the Prince Henry Cliff Path. That was where Leura Falls goes over the edge. He was going to send me a photo.

This all made perfect sense as I strode back the way we had come. As it turned out, I got it completely wrong. He did go on to Mount Solitary. He didn't go to see Leura Falls, or any of the other waterfalls that grace this region.

We boarded the Scenic Railway to ride up the steepest railway track in the world back up to the Scenic World complex on the cliff top. We caught a bus to bring us back to the hotel.

I had forgotten to take my phone with me when we set out that morning. There was a message from Ian Collis asking me to get in touch. When we spoke, he asked if I could come to a meeting at Katoomba Police Station at about six o'clock that Sunday evening. This sounded bad news. Either they had found a body or they were calling off the search. If they had found him alive they surely would have said so. If they were scaling things down, I would have to try to persuade them to keep going for a few more days. Especially now I could tell them about the waterfall idea. I was bracing myself for bad news.

Chapter Eight

The Despair

The ominous summons to a meeting with Ian Collis at six o'clock was not the only message that was waiting for me back at the hotel. Ann, manager of the Youth Hostel, had left a note to ask if I wished to meet someone who had spoken with Jamie before he went missing. Jeff and I arranged to pop across at half past five. We were also due to meet up with Debbie and Peter. Debbie was an English lass who had settled down in a neighbouring town to Katoomba. She was a good friend of Jean's sister-in-law from the time she lived in the old country. Now she was married to Peter, who was an Australian. Jean suggested we meet up because Debbie knew a lot of the Park Rangers. She might be able to provide an inside view of the progress of the search. She had spoken to Jean about the many missing hikers who go missing for a few days then turn up exhausted but unscathed. It would cheer me up to talk to her.

We had a busy evening ahead of us.

The meeting at the hostel came first. Ann introduced us to Raoul, a twenty three year old Dutchman. He was a fine looking young man, tall and well-built with jet black hair and dark eyes. He didn't look Dutch. He may have been was partly Timorese or Javan. He spoke of Jamie bubbling over with enthusiasm for his adventure in the bush. Raoul claimed to have been concerned about such reckless confidence in a lad unfamiliar with the Australian bush. Hindsight? Maybe, but I recognised the mood that Rauol described. Jamie could be cocksure of himself, irritatingly talkative when he was excited about something. Jamie had been proud of his excellent performance orienteering through Epping Forest for the Duke of Edinburgh. So it was a case of 'bring on the next challenge'. The walk to Mount Solitary had been suggested by another backpacker staying at the hostel. A Canadian named Matthew. The Police were trying to trace this young man, who had moved on to Thailand by the time Jamie's disappearance became known.

It was Raoul who had noticed that Jamie's phone had been left untouched and on-charge for three days and it was this that led to the realisation that he had not been back since Friday morning. Ann explained that no-one had raised the alarm when he failed to show up for his pre-booked trip to Jenolan Caves on the Saturday because this happened quite frequently. People change their minds or forget what they've booked or simply can't get out of bed in time. The papers had misreported this as the initial moment that the penny had dropped.

I asked Raoul and Ann if I could take their picture. It would mean a lot to Jean to see the people who had been the last to see our son, especially as it was Rauol who raised the alarm. Ann is clearly distressed in the picture I took. Raoul has broken into a broad cheesy grin, as if he is on holiday.

Over the road at Katoomba Cop Shop, we met Area Commander Tony McWhirter for the first time. Ian Collis was yawning and he seemed about to nod off during the meeting, so it was Tony who did the talking. A family of English holidaymakers had set out on a bushwalk the previous day and failed to get back when it got dark. Ian had been called out in the early hours to co-ordinate a search for them. They were eventually led out of the bush, safe and well, at five in the morning. More lost Pommies. As Lady

Bracknell almost said, "To lose one may be counted a misfortune, to lose the whole bloody family starts to look like carelessness".

I got in the first shot.

"I'm worried that you are going to say you're calling off the search".

I was dreading this. Of course, I still hoped he would be found and for that reason alone I needed the search to go on till there was not the slightest hope Jamie might still be alive, but I also felt Jean, in her grief, would seek someone to blame, someone who hadn't done everything she thought they should have done to find her wonderful son. She knew he was out there. If they called the search off, it would be because I had not insisted that they keep looking for him - I had been too negative about his chances, I had let the police off the hook.

I was a lot less confident about how much influence I could bring to bear, but I would do my best. I knew they would do their best to accommodate my feelings but, ultimately, it was a matter of expert medical advice about how long Jamie could possibly still be alive. Thankfully it was okay. I didn't need to beg them to keep searching - for Jean's sake, for Jamie's sake, for my sake, to save me from having to endure the next ten years of blame for a decision that I had no part in making.

"No. We're not at that stage yet".

That settled both worries. There would be no 'yet' if he had been found dead. Tony was a big, bearded bloke, kind and courteous, likeable and approachable.

The reason they needed to see me was to explain the procedure if, as he obviously hoped would not be the case, they were unable to locate Jamie during the following week. He said they were planning a specialist search of the Leura Cascades on Monday, using their toughest and most highly trained team of searchers. Then there would be a big effort on Tuesday, using over seventy volunteers. After that the search would be scaled back. The choppers would keep searching until Friday. I could not complain. I told them about my waterfall theory; the pattern of trips he'd taken with his dad, the eclipse and the dead dictators. I said I'd been on the Ruined Castle track and there was nothing there to do him harm. It was an eerie co-incidence, but the search round the Leura Cascades was just the sort of thing that should flow from my speculation.

They were taking expert medical advice about how long Jamie could realistically be expected to survive in the relevant circumstances. I broke in to emphasise that they should not take the supposed cold weather into account.

"He's like me. That boy could run to the South Pole in his underpants".

Tony smiled ruefully. He must have known I would talk up Jamie's chances. It could have been a lot worse. I could have been hysterical. If they'd told Jean they were thinking of calling the search off, she would have flown at them.

I was pleased to hear that the search was still going on. One factor that had to be borne in mind was that they were largely dependent on volunteers, mostly members of New South Wales Rural Fire Service. These wonderful men and women gave up their time and sweated labour out of a humane concern for the life of another human being. On that very Sunday, there had been serious casualties among the searchers. A man had collapsed from exhaustion and a woman had broken her arm. Once it got to the stage when it was no longer a search for a living person, it was neither fair nor practicable to continue calling upon the services of these unselfish, unpaid volunteers when everyone realised that they were looking for a body.

"Looking for a body". The phrase was chilling. Tony reiterated that they had not got to that stage 'yet'.

Tony went on to explain about the legal implications of a person missing for a long time, presumed dead. In theory, it was necessary to wait seven years for someone to be declared legally dead in the absence of a body. During that time there must be no evidence of activity, such as bank withdrawals or reliable sightings. It was permissible for a coroner to allow for a shorter period of absence if they felt there were good reasons to do so. In the kind of case under discussion, there was likely to be an inquest soon after a year had gone by. If the coroner was satisfied that my son was no longer alive, we would then be issued with a death certificate.

"Yes. You will probably be required to attend and give evidence".

I could only sit there and stare. Jeff was asking the questions. I cannot blame these thoroughly decent, dedicated men for what they were telling me. They were not doing it to upset me. They were simply doing their duty. I had to understand. My son was dead. They were doing the decent thing by keeping up the search so long as any lingering smidgeon of hope remained that he was still alive out there. But they believed he was dead. They needed me to understand. To make provision. To prepare myself for the worst.

And all I could think was the same as everyone thinks when death comes to them or the one they love. "Why me?"

For me, there was a sharper edge to this self-pity. First Irenka, now Jamie. I'm not perfect, but, dear God, I try my best to be a good man, a good father. I don't deserve to be kicked in the teeth two times running, to spend ten years of my twenties and thirties saddened by the violent death of the woman I loved and now, the years to come, my old age, to be stricken by the loss of someone else who meant the world to me. Just when I thought he was off to university, off to make me even more proud of him. He was such a brilliant son.

"What we need you to do is come back here just before you go home and give us a statement. With your permission, we would also like to take a sample of your DNA".

I am writing this down in October. My son has thankfully been found. Yes, we have not spoken for a while. There are tears in my eyes as I write.

The meeting with Debbie and Peter was a good idea. They could not tell me anything about the search, nor could any uplifting tale of the other hikers' survival wash away the brutal reality of what I had been told, but their company gave me something to take my mind off the misery which had steadily engulfed me after each passing, fruitless day: the massive unrewarded effort by foot patrols, dog handlers, motor bikes, choppers. Still no news.

They collected us from the hotel and drove us to their favourite Indian Restaurant. We talked about other things. Not about the search. I liked Debbie, but I have no recollection of anything I said to her or she said to me. I remember Jeff asking Pete about the test match. That's all. My mind was elsewhere.

The following morning we took the Scenic Railway down to the path beneath the cliffs. This railway had been built to serve the mines at the base of the sandstone, to haul up coal for transfer to the main railway back to the coast. It claims to be the steepest railway track in the world. It was, of course, cable operated, with cages to stop passengers banging their heads on the overhanging rocks. The carriages were articulated in the up and down direction to cope with the sinuosity of the track, more like a roller coaster than a railway.

This time I wanted to move eastward along the base of the cliffs, away from the route to Ruined Castle. It was a path that led across the various creeks that tumble over the edge of the Katoomba-Leura Plateau - Katoomba Cascades, Linda Falls, Leura Cascades and Gordon Falls. Anyone of these could be the waterfall where my son had got in trouble. We would be following a path known as 'The Federal Pass Walking Track'. It was a path that had been cut from the talus slope in the thirties to provide work for the otherwise unemployed. Another path ran along the top of the cliffs high above us. This was the Prince Henry Cliff Walk. Unlike my son, we could consult the excellent Department of Lands four centimetres to the kilometre maps of Katoomba and the Jamison Valley, with a satellite camera image of the area on the reverse. I could see that the Federal Pass Track came to an end near the base of the Leura Cascades. I wanted to go further, hoping to crash on through the trackless bush until I reached Gordon Creek.

Astonishingly, when Jamie eventually came back into my life, he said he had believed that he was close to the Gordon Falls at the time he was, in fact, lost in the Cedar Creek region. He had been completely disorientated. He had mistaken the cliffs on the far side of Mount Solitary for a headland of the main plateau, which was behind them from his then point of view. This was the young man who had orienteered his way through Epping Forest with flying colours but, by the time of this error, his judgment had been compromised by hunger and anxiety. This time, he didn't have a decent map to navigate by.

We exited the tourist bubble at the base of the railway and were soon walking along under the cliff. It was a sunshiny day and although we were low down compared with the cliff above, we could still see for miles down the valley to the south. There was Mount Solitary and there was the Narrow Neck Plateau pushing out to meet it. The lesser excrescence poking up from the tree cover about half way between the two was Ruined Castle. The rest of the valley was undulating forest as far as the eye could see, with a glimmer of Lake Burragorang near the horizon.

This track was nowhere near as busy as the one to the castle, but parts of it were a delight, with tall gums, exotic tree ferns - parrots screeching and flapping in the sunshine. Jeff has done a lot of bushwalking, but he said this was as good as it gets. As we progressed round the base of The Three Sisters and then followed the cliff line north towards Linda and Leura Falls, we noticed something odd about the tree cover. It seemed to thin out in a line parallel to the track and about one hundred yards down slope. I left the track and made my way downhill to satisfy my curiosity. I expected to find a stream or marsh. In fact it was a vehicular access track, suitable for four-wheel drive. I found this astonishing. I had assumed from the height and steepness of the cliffs that only walkers could pick their way down to the valley floor, using steps hacked out of the rock face or using the cable operated cliff railway. Yet here was a track clearly intended for the use of vehicular traffic - two parallel strips of bare earth with a strip of grass in between. I traced the route of the track on the map as it snaked down through the valley and up the cliff onto Kings Tableland, not far from the search base camp. When we reached Leura Falls, it was clear that the stream had been modified by civil engineering work. The track must have been cut to facilitate this. It was something of a revelation to me to find that the impenetrable forest was not, after all, a trackless primordial desert. There were not just paths for walkers but also vehicular access for hydraulic engineers and power line riggers.

When we got to the end of the path, I wanted to go on. For my own safety, Jeff would remain on the west side of the Leura Creek. There was a small picnic area nearby, with a rusty, corrugated iron shelter dedicated to Lady Carrington. I picked my way across the boulders that broke up the torrential flow of the creek then carried on into the trackless scrub on the far side. It was tough going, with fallen rocks and trees and lots of 'mallee scrub', more bushes than trees. I was scratched and whipped by the branches, snagged by trailing vines. My hat was battered and frequently displaced as I crashed on through. I knew from the map that, if I kept going parallel to the cliff, I would arrive on the right bank of Gordon Creek. I had seen no red ribbons, so maybe I was the first to come this way since Jamie vanished. I shouted out his name in case he lay injured nearby.

I soon heard the sound of foaming water and then emerged at the water's edge. Again I was astonished. Instead of flowing across my path from left to right the water was rushing the other way, as if heading back to the cliff. That was impossible. It took a few minutes to dawn on me what had happened. I had not reached Gordon Creek; I had crossed the Leura then found my way through the scrub to encounter the same creek further downstream. While I imagined myself working along the base of the cliff, the lie of the land had been pushing me steadily down the slope until I had progressed in a bow-shaped curve, with Leura Creek as the bow-string. I followed the Leura downstream until it joined the Gordon, crossed back over to the western side and followed a path upstream to find the point where I had originally crossed over. I was able to recognise some of the concrete structures that lay beside the place where I had crossed but I still had to retrace my steps after I missed the path leading away from the creek to where Jeff was waiting. I had been away from him for only about three quarters of an hour yet, in that time, I had missed one path and become confused about my location elsewhere, despite my having a good map and the adjacent cliff to navigate by. The experience had brought it home to me how easy it was to become disorientated in the bush. It also showed how the gradient subtly pushes you away from a straight line path, in a direction you might not intend to go. Each time I came upon an obstruction, either a large boulder or impenetrable bush, it was easier to go round it by stepping downhill. Then I would press on at this lower level until the next obstruction sent me even further down the slope. It was these downward detours that had accumulated to bring about my unplanned return to the stream I'd crossed only twenty minutes earlier.

Jeff and I retraced our steps back to the Scenic Railway and emerged muddy and hungry among the crowds and squealing children up top. It had been another frustrating day's effort with absolutely nothing to show for it. I was hungry, exhausted and fearful about my son. I wanted to sit down and eat at the Scenic World restaurant, but Jeff said he preferred to try a small café he had spotted on the way to Scenic World. So we collected the van and drove about half a mile to this place. I was a bit irritated by the need to travel a bit further before I could sit down and eat, but I lumped it for Jeff's sake. The café turned out to be a rather twee sort of place with homemade cakes and homemade soup of the day. There was meat pie on the menu but when I asked to have one, the lady said she only cooked at lunchtime. It was just before four o'clock.

"How about soup and a roll?"

"We're out of rolls at the moment".

For this I had walked away from the restaurant at Scenic World.

I laid into Jeff.

"I said this was a lousy idea!"

I left my brother munching on a biscuit and holding his polystyrene cup of coffee, while I sped back to Scenic World. I waited an eternity in the queue and then, just before I reached the front, I got stuck behind one of those idiots who have some piffling query to air and every time you think they've finished and you draw breath to speak, they have to say something else to the poor girl behind the counter and this goes on and on till you wish you had an ice-pick to smash into the back of this bloke's head. Finally, I got to speak to the jolly blonde with pigtails.

"Can I have the meat pie and chips, please?"

"I'm afraid the pies are off today".

"What about a bacon, lettuce and tomato sandwich?"

"I'm sorry, we can't do that either. I can offer you a..."

What the f____ was the matter with this country? We're talking about one sodding meat pie here. Not soufflé. Not crêpe f_____g suzette!

"Look, just bloody forget it, will you!" I stormed off.

As I said in the last chapter., I was uncivil. I apologise.

I returned to Jeff and he offered me his packet of crisps.

There was one more place we had to check out. I wanted to see the Prince Henry Cliff Path. The text message about this path had been my introduction to the place names of Katoomba. I knew a lot more now: Mount Solitary, Narrow Neck, Ruined Castle, Leura and Jamison - sonorous evocative syllables that would be etched into my brain forever. It was late in the afternoon and the middle of the southern winter. I parked the van in a car park next to the Leura River, close to the point where it tumbles over the cliff. We made our way onto the path. The path was steep in places, with viewpoints over the falls and out over the valley. There were metal barriers to stop you from falling over the edge, if you were sensible. Jamie was reckoned to have come this way on the morning he disappeared, to watch the sunrise. He had then gone back to the hostel before setting out for the last time, stepping off the face of the planet. When I heard about the tradition of watching the sunrise from this cliff, I was puzzled. The view faced south, not east. Raoul had explained it to me. It is the rays of the eastern sun moving across the surface of the delicately coloured stone that creates the enchantment, changing shadows into light, dissolving away the morning mist.

We were there shortly before sunset. In gathering gloom we wandered round the amphitheatrical embayment that enclosed the cascades. I could look across to the steep cliffs on the opposite side. There were thousands of trees lined up along the edge, craning and straining over the edge, inviting the incautious to lean out for a better view, maybe rest a hand upon a convenient branch, a rotten branch. We moved on. Beneath an overhanging crag I sat down and sobbed. Drips of water oozed from crazes in the face of the rock. Jeff moved away, leaving me to let it out.

I was convinced that it was near here that he had lost his life. He had been dead all along. Dead since before anyone knew he had gone missing. It was down to me. Innocent things we'd done together drew him here to die. That trek up to Aber Falls on the North Welsh coast back in 2007 had sowed the seeds of his demise, fated my son to come here and try to take a picture for me. He had the message ready on the mobile phone, then changed his mind, intending to come back with a proper camera, to get the best picture, to show off to his dad. The Ruined Castle walk was meant to follow, but he never got his chance to set out. And that was how he died. For me. My wonderful, darling son.

It was too dark to keep going. We trekked back to where I'd parked the van.

Sitting on a bench in darkness, I called Jean. I told her where I was. The Prince Henry Cliff Walk. I told her the police had told us to prepare for the worst. Jean was gasping for her breath, puffing on her inhaler. She struggled with every word she spoke.

"No! You go back and tell them he's alive. You're too negative. You have to get them to keep looking!"

"Please Jean, I don't need this right now. I've seen the cliffs. I've seen how many people there are round here. You can't just wander in circles and no-one sees you. We're still searching. The police are still searching but they don't think he's alive anymore!"

I was crying and she was sobbing and gasping for breath.

She told me she wanted me to bring home the maps to show all the places where they had searched for him. I was dreading this. She was looking for someone to blame. "Why didn't they search here?" she'd ask when she saw the map. "That's where he was!"

Weeks later, when Jamie had come back to her and she could smugly tease me about how she'd been right all along when everyone else, especially me, had got it wrong, she denied she'd asked for the map to find someone to blame. She had wanted to see it so Gary could fly over. He would search the places they'd missed. That I'd missed. He would find his brother, her son, and bring him home to her.

Chapter Nine

The Agony

On the morning of the following day, I drove the car to a liquor store and purchased seventy-two bottles of beer to load into the back of the Hiace. Then I popped into a nearby garden centre to buy a bit of string. There was no string for sale, but when I explained to the grave and dignified man who ran the place that I needed it to draw a circle so I could carve a Tudor rose in memory of the son I'd lost in the bush, he gave me a piece out of a tray of bits and pieces for his own use. I went over to *Coles* and bought hammer , chisel and rechargeable drill with two sets of drill bits. I was running out of clean shirts and my heel had been blistered by my walking boots, so I threw in a bottle green t-shirt and a cheap pair of trainers. Jeff came back from the high street with two red roses and a thick red candle.

We popped back to our hotel so I could put the drill on charge and then I went across to the police station to advise them that I would be back that evening to make my statement and provide a sample of my DNA. Then it was back to the search base for the last time.

Ian Collis was pleased to see us, as he had some positive news. Jamie had been identified by a couple of walkers down at Ruined Castle on the morning of the 3rd. The couple had just come forward. They said the youth they met had been dressed in a *Prada* t-shirt. This was something that had not been publicised. Indeed, even I had not known he was dressed in *Prada* up until this time. The last image of Jamie, a video capture of his leaving the hostel, had shown him from the rear, but I knew for certain that he possessed such a shirt. I had made a joke about it two months earlier. So he hadn't fallen from the cliffs at Leura Cascades after all. The witnesses had spoken to Jamie and he had told them he was pressing on to Mount Solitary. I was wrong about that too.

We left the beer in the tent for the volunteers. Ian said even more had come than he had anticipated. They had about ninety men and women to send out. They would need to fight over the seventy two bottles. The new information confirmed Mount Solitary as the most promising area to search. I did not tell Ian I was going to carve a memorial for my son out at 'Ruined Castle'. He would doubtless tell me that I was desecrating a national monument, maybe detain me on some sort of criminal intent charge.

My latest speculation to account for Jamie's continued absence was that he may have reached the top of Solitary just as it was getting dark. Rather than hunker down for an uncomfortable night out in the bush, he had tried to pick his way down in the fading light. He was, after all, keen to be back for his morning excursion to the Jenolan Caves. In the darkness he mistook the way and fell to his doom. There was a King of Scotland who fell to his death from the sea-cliffs on the coast of Fife. He had been riding through the night to lie alongside his newly wedded wife. People make light of risks when transfixed by their wish to fulfill a settled arrangement.

After this day there would never be another mass search for Jamie. If he was still alive, this was to be our last realistic chance to find him. Tomorrow they would, in Tony's words, be using choppers to 'drop specialist teams into remote and inaccessible locations'. If these places were so hard to get into that they could only be accessed by chopper, it begged the question as to how they reckoned Jamie might have ended up there. The answer was not hard to figure out. They thought that he too had dropped down from the sky. As for me and my brother, we were no longer searching. I had come to accept that I was unlikely to see my son alive again, if at all. I was looking for closure. I had to go back into the bush but, this time, with no real thought of finding him. He was out there somewhere and I just needed to be as near as I could be to say goodbye. The only comfort in this sad business was that he had found such a magnificent place to lay his bones - a place where the morning mists wreath round soaring cliffs, a place where lyre birds call and the trees grow high. A grave fit for a god.

We hung around for a while so that the drill battery would be juiced up for the task ahead. Then we packed our bags and checked out of the hotel. We popped over to the hostel to thank Ann for her help and support and to say goodbye. Then it was off to find The Golden Stairs and walk out to Ruined Castle for the third and last time. The small car park at the top of The Stairs was crowded with jeeps and trucks and minibuses, Police, Rural Fire Service and an ambulance. There was even a camera crew. It was not easy to find a room to park but we found a spot alongside the road a short distance down from the car park. I told the Search and Rescue guys that there was a bottle of beer for each of them at the base camp. I shook their hands and told them that this boy was worth all the effort they were putting in to find him. They knew that, they said. They would find him, they said.

The camera crew followed me down The Golden Stairs, racing on to overtake me each time I passed so that they got another shot of my worried face as I came toward them. This carried on till the path became too steep and they went back to the top. We met a family walking along the track with a boy of about five years old tagging along. I explained who I was and asked if it was okay to take a photo so I could show Jamie's mother how safe it was down here. There was nothing to fear on this track. No place to vanish without being found, wander in circles till you die alone. It was not like the Sahara Desert or the Great North Woods. They let me have the family picture. The kid looks annoyed.

There are two significant outcrops of rock on the elongated mound that makes up 'Ruined Castle'. When we came this way on Sunday, Jeff and I had split up by the first outcrop. I had made my way straight down the side of the hill back to the main path, just to see how hard or easy it was to travel 'off *piste*'. Jeff had carried on past the second outcrop and down the path that rejoined the main track further along from where it had originally branched off. He had then tracked back to join me at the spot where I had emerged from my own, steeper but shorter descent through the trees.

I was looking for a rock face out of the rain so that the surface would not be eroded away. There was a promising overhang on the side of the first outcrop, with a reasonably flat, almost vertical face on which to work. Jeff said that there was a bigger pile of rock further along. Maybe there would be a better place for Jamie's memorial. On investigation of Jeff's outcrop, I found another place where the rock was protected from the elements, but this flat surface was horizontal, like a table. I reckoned it was better than the other site, mainly because it was more discrete. The other place was in view of anyone passing along the path. It would also be more like an altar, on which I could place the candle. The chosen spot looked south-westerly, down into the valley of Cedar Creek.

As I set to work with the drill, I soon realised that it was not possible to carve this rock as delicately as I would have wished. The drill was slow and underpowered compared with a mains powered device. I had to forget about carving a Tudor rose to set alongside his name and I had to edit down my words to save time. I could only gouge and drill a crude track through the flaky surface of the rock. I scratched out his name, date of birth and the date he walked out the youth hostel. I was worried that someone might find the memorial and mistake it for a last, desperate message from the boy himself, so I also carved 'my son'. I would have chosen to write 'my beloved son' and 'in memory of' if there had been more time and more flat rock to work with. I also wrote 'lost' rather than 'missing'. The result is uncharacteristically laconic for me, but time was short, the rock friable and uncooperative. It would have to do. The 'o' shapes of the zeroes, eight and nine all end up shaped like diamonds rather than circles. The effort left me with enhanced admiration for the stone carvers of medieval cathedrals, Maya step pyramids or Ancient Egyptian tombs. Then there were those big Assyrian statues of bearded men with the bodies of bulls which we had seen together, Jamie, Clair and me, when we went to the British Museum, when I was a Sunday afternoon dad and my son was five years old. I was using modern, well-tempered chisels and drill bits but my results were crude and compromised compared with the exquisite products of those nameless ancient masons.

The weather was a lot colder than at any time since the night I'd arrived in Oz, so I put on a sweater for once. There were gusts of wind that blew dust in my face and eddies that twirled the litter of cellophane and cardboard. From time to time, someone would come up to the rock and find me hacking away at this prominent feature of their National Park. Jeff would quietly tell them it was okay. It was just a crazy old man grieving for his lost son. They stared at me and went on their way. After a couple of hours I'd done as much as I could do. We would need an hour to get back down the path and another half hour to make it back to the top of the cliff. I had to be back in Katoomba by six to make my statement and donate my DNA. I gathered up the bits and pieces and all the litter and put them in a bag. Most of the drill bits were blunt by this time. I was hoping to donate the drill to a charity shop in Katoomba but, as there was no time for that, Jeff took it back to Perth. It was too slow for the job. I had ended up using the bits as scrapers. The final message read 'Jamie Neale b 21.11.89 lost 3.7.09 my son'.

I found a place to bury the rose. I had in mind the Rupert Brooke line about some corner of a foreign field that is 'forever England'. Perhaps I should have read a poem, maybe 'Drummer Hodge' by Thomas Hardy. Poetry is the new liturgy at funerals these days. I had read *'My Country'* by Dorothea MacKellar at my father's passing, two years before. *'Drummer*

Hodge', describes the final resting place of a boy soldier cut down in the Boer War, how he lies so far from home beneath strange stars, *'his breast and brain grow to some Southern tree'*. The poem featured in Alan Bennett's *'The History Boys'*, so I knew Jamie had heard this poem. I thought about this too late to do anything about it.

I phoned Jean and set the candle down on the rock. It had to be lit several times and moved around to find a sheltered spot, out of the breeze. I placed the remaining rose across the words I had carved and looked out across Cedar Creek Valley. I had not planned anything to say. Nothing written down.

"I'm sorry, Jamie. We did our best. We're so sorry we can't bring you back with us. I loved you so much. I wanted you to go on to make me so proud of you. I know I should have told you before you flew away from us. I've got to go home tomorrow. We'll never forget you, Jamie".

Then I slumped back and stared in silence for a while with my hands clasped. I was not praying. I was bitter at any god who could do something like this. Then it was done. This was as good a funeral as we were going to have. Time was getting on and I had to leave this place and attend to the rest of the procedures that would mark his passing.

Jeff had gone on ahead to leave me with my last thoughts at this place where my son had vanished off the face of the earth. When I arrived down by the base of the hill, back at the old mine railway track, Jeff was in trouble. He had twisted his ankle between rocks on the way down. We had a long walk back to the Golden Stairs and a strenuous climb to complete when we got there. He was able to hobble along, but suffered at every step.

On the way back we were overtaken by a file of about forty search volunteers in their yellow jackets. The men ranged in age from teenagers to greybeards but they were lean and fit and moving at twice our speed. They were such a fine body of men you almost expected them to burst into song like Welsh miners walking home from a pit in the thirties. It brought a lump to my throat to see them and know that they were doing so much for me and my son.

"Any news?"

"I'm afraid not," said the man leading his searchers home. I shook the hands of as many men as I could. The leader came back and apologised to me for not realising that I was Jamie's father. He said how sorry he was for not being able to bring better news.

I told him about Jeff's ankle. He offered to arrange an airlift out if Jeff was unable to make it. Jeff said he would be okay. A couple of guys were delegated to stay with us while the rest of the troop moved on. Jeff got his ankle strapped up in the ambulance at the top of the Golden Stairs. I thanked as many of the men as I could for their kindness on behalf of me and my family. It was such a crying shame that we hadn't found him. They would have to get back to the search base before all the beer was gone.

Then Jeff and I drove off in the van, back to Katoomba town and the police station where the next stage of my disengagement was about to take place.

I was sat in front of a lady inspector while she debriefed me about all that had gone on since I arrived in Katoomba five days earlier. It took a lot of paper and a lot of time. I was feeling sorry for Jeff who was just waiting outside while I went through the process, with nothing for him to do but sorrow. Even after the statement seemed all typed up and ready to go, I had to read it all through and there were bits she hadn't understood that had to be changed, or explained or added. I knew this statement would become part of the evidence at any future inquest so it was important to get it right.

Then it was time to sort out the DNA sample. I was led into another room and sat where the video camera could see me. The lady hadn't done this before, so she was checking the instructions in a manual to get the procedure right. There were lots of things to sign and I had to signify my consent and that I understood by loudly saying 'Yes, I do' to about ten different statements before eventually she handed me a white plastic lollipop and told me to scrape it against the inside of my cheek.

The lollipop had a rough, pumice-like surface to pick up my skin cells and their DNA. She pressed this gooey, saliva-soaked stick onto the designated sticky bit of paper then popped it into a plastic bag and handed it back to me. For keeps. That was a surprise.

Then we were off home. While Jeff picked up fish and chips in the high street, I looked through the bits of paper in my pocket for the phone number of the guy who'd met me outside the police station when I'd arrived the previous Friday. I felt sorry for the way I'd kept putting him off, when the coverage by the *'Telegraph'* had been so good, so sympathetic. I had been handed lots of bits of paper over the last four days, but I found one that said *'Telegraph'* and gave the number a call. Tim Verotel was at home and I could hear a baby gurgling in the background. This was the first time I ventured onto the slippery slope of actually courting the attention of the media. I wanted people to know about the shrine I'd carved into the rocks of 'Ruined Castle'.

Maybe people could start up a cairn next to it, and I could come back one day and see how many rocks had been added. Hikers would stop by and maybe say a little prayer in memory of a promising and thoughtful young man who came to Australia so full of life and touched the hearts of so many after he failed to come back. The next time I spoke to Tim was at the Blue Mountain Hospital after Jamie was found. He was not the heavy-metal roadie look-alike.

Then it was on the road and back to Sydney. At about ten pm we headed east on the Great Western Highway. I tried to pick up something to listen to on the radio but nothing seemed to engage me so we ended up driving in silence. Mindful of all those tolls, I tried to avoid the motorway, but that localised inability to find any useful direction sign continued to afflict my progress. We ended up bowling along a motorway all the way to Sydney. Every now and then a mysterious message would appear overhead telling me that some kind of tracking device should now be operating to register our passage. I had no idea what it was trying to tell me. There were signs about off-road toll booths too, but they all specified 'no cash' so we just kept going. Just before the end we found a toll booth that accepted cash. I was pleased that I would not be troubling the car-hire company with unpaid tolls. In fact I got two lots of fines through the post, topped up with charges on my credit card for admin fees on behalf of the hire company. I still haven't a clue how I was meant to avoid this.

I had booked a room at the Formule 1 hotel. We got there about midnight, navigating by the lights of the Krispy Kreme. Jeff took a shower. I went to bed. I briefly turned on the TV. It was 'Little Britain'. I turned off the telly and went to sleep.

Chapter Ten

The Ecstasy

On the morning of what I assumed would be my last day in Australia, my first task of the day was to work out how to put diesel into the Hiace van. Luckily I managed to catch a builder working on a new wing for the hotel just as he was getting stuff out of his own Hiace. He showed me the lever that operated the flap. I was obliged to top up the tank before I returned it to the hire company.

Jeff's ankle was a little better and we discussed whether to pass the time down by the harbour before we caught our flights back to where we came from. I just wasn't in the mood. He came with me to drop off the van, as he wanted to get a copy of *"The Australian'* to read at the airport.

The area we walked through after we had handed over the van was a run-down part of Sydney, with car lots, sweatshops and dilapidated buildings, some in use, some not. One that definitely was in use was a pie factory. A café was latched on to the side – with a menu consisting entirely of pies. This was quite unbelievable. I had spent a good deal of the last five days yearning after the Great Australian Meat Pie, to be fobbed off with nothing tastier than shrugged shoulders and a barramundi fish. Was this to be God's last little joke against me in the throes of my Jobian anguish? A providential pie in the face jest just as I finally abandoned hope of seeing my son or breaching pie-crust till I touched base in Blighty?

Despite having breakfasted at the Formule 1, we had plenty of time to kill, so, like Simple Simon, we went inside to ask the pieman or, as happened to be the case, piewoman, "May we have a pie?"

Or, at any rate, "I'll have the beef and burgundy with peas and mash, please".

There was yet another copy of the *'Telegraph'*. I do believe that this tabloid could probably devote its entire print run to the catering trade and still sell enough copies to make a profit. Jamie was no longer front page. On page eighteen there was a photo of a lonely figure standing on a cliff edge, gazing out over the vast cliff-girt expanse of the Jamison Valley. The headline read 'Somewhere in here a tourist is missing'. The reporters were Charles Miranda and Tim Vollmer. There were a few other customers in the place. The pielady apparently knew these other customers - she sat at the same table while they ate. Nobody paid us any mind. In better circumstances, it would have been great but now even this last boon of a beef and burgundy pie was not going to lift my spirits.

I recalled the last time I had dined like this with my brother. Jeff had come back to the UK for the first time since immigrating to Perth, We ended up at Nathan's pie and mash shop in the shadow of West Ham's Football Ground. This craving for pie and mash, with green, parsley-flavoured gravy, is an East End affectation passed through our Cockney mother's genes. Jeff posed for a photo beneath the monumental bronze of Bobby Moore, Martin Peters and that same Geoff Hurst whose misspelt name he now claimed as his own. They are holding up the World Cup. Jeff offers up his meat pie to the camera.

From the pie shop, it was back to the hotel, collect our bags and catch the shuttle bus for the short ride to the international airport. I had about five hours to wait for my three pm departure. Jeff would wave me off then transfer to the domestic terminal for his own flight back to Perth. We were so early that there were not yet any staff on duty at the check-in desk and no one else waiting around. After an hour or so, an all-female family of Chinese mothers and daughters arrived and sat behind us. I was mournful but not openly distraught. I tried to believe that there was still hope that he would turn up, but I was rational enough to know that most times we don't get what we hope for. I wondered how long it would be before even this last flicker of hope expired and I accepted that my son's rich involvement with my life had ended. I talked about Jamie and what a wonderful son he'd been to me. Jeff was wise enough to listen without saying too much back. To pass the time and divert our thoughts, he commenced the crossword on the back of *'The Australian'*.

Within the hour, we had cracked just about every clue. My mobile phone bleeped to alert me about a text. The message was an automatic alert that I had missed a call and that there was a voice message waiting for me. I don't know why I didn't get the call. I may not have heard the ring tone in the vast, crowded departures hall, or maybe the signal strength had been too weak to get through. Some papers reported that I got the news that Jamie was okay by text message. What happened was I got a text about a voice-message that told me to phone Area Commander Tony McWhirter to hear some 'good news'.

Of course, as soon as I heard the phrase 'good news', I knew that Jamie was okay. He had been found alive. I did not know how, or by whom or what condition he was in but I knew he was alive and that was all that mattered. He hadn't fallen off a cliff.

I was shaking with excitement. I had to write down the phone number and translate it into international dialing code to phone from my UK mobile. It meant I had the pen in my hand as I rang. I was to be asked many times about the words we exchanged when I got through to Tony. I have no doubt it must have been one of the most wonderful moments of his own distinguished career. For myself, I cannot recall the exact words that passed between us. The voicemail message had already told me what I wanted to know. Incredibly, while waiting on the phone, the answer to the final crossword clue clicked in my head. I held the pen, so I scribbled it down quickly across a space on the paper in case Jeff claimed he got there before me. The answer to the most challenging cryptic clue in *'The Australian'* crossword for Wednesday the 15th of July was 'argument'.

Tony told me they had Jamie and that he was okay. He was so relieved I hadn't boarded my flight. A car would come to pick me up at the airport to run me to a helicopter. I would then fly back to Katoomba for a reunion with the son I'd given up for dead.

"My boy's been found!" I shouted. So bad are the acoustics of a huge and high departure complex that no one took any notice. I wanted the world to know that Jamie was safe. I assumed that everyone had heard about him. I had to tell someone the good news. I thrust out the crumpled *"Telegraph'* from the previous Wednesday to the Chinese family sitting behind me. "That's my boy. He's been found. My boy's been found!"

They smiled and nodded and clucked with pleasure at the excellent news, as most people do when confronted by a madman. Then it was time to phone Jean and text the people who had sent so many messages of support to me in my time of worry.

I had told Tony my location - check in number J, if that makes sense. Jeff said he would not be coming back to Katoomba with me. I suspect he realised the fuss that would greet me there. I asked him to sort out the cancellation of my three o'clock flight to Bangkok. I heard my name announced on the loudspeaker system, either Richard Cass or British Gas. It was so hard to make out. Jeff was elsewhere, so I had to haul my bags about half a mile to an enquiries desk to find out what had been said. It was, inevitably, a message on behalf of the police to say that they had arrived to pick me up at my original location. I thanked Jeff for all his help and carried my bags to the squad car.

While I was in the car, Gary phoned from the UK to share the news. He said one of the reporters said Jamie's story would be worth thousands of pounds.

I told him to shut up and f-off. I found this distasteful at a time like this. I was also worried that, if the police were listening, they would assume it had all been a moneymaking stunt. I now look back on this intemperate outburst as an unheeded warning about how quickly my temper could be aroused when my bloodstream was primed with adrenaline. Then we were in the air and scudding across the suburbs and then the bush all the way back to Katoomba. We landed right outside the hospital. There were already about fifty gentlefolk of the press, flashing their still cameras and homing in on me with their video cameras as I was escorted at a brisk walk into the sanctum of the hospital and down the various corridors to the intensive care facility where my son was waiting. Doors were swung back for us and security men stood aside ready to stand in position as soon as we passed. It was like the progress of a champion boxer through the crowd to the ring where he is gonna get pummeled.

Then I beheld my son.

He looked terrible. He was propped up in bed with a drip in his arm. His teeth and cheekbones had never seemed so prominent. The eyebrows and chinstrap beard were bushier than ever. Even his nose appeared shriveled and shrunk. He looked like Mr Tumnus, the faun from 'The Lion, the Witch and the Wardrobe'. Perhaps shaggy, goatish limbs lay concealed beneath the blankets. He had the eyes of a crazy castaway.

But it was him.

I smiled and hugged him. It's so bloody marvelous to see you again.

He smiled back, almost painfully.

I couldn't stop myself. "You steeewpid, steeewpid boy! You put me and your mum through hell. But it's brilliant, so good to have you back!"

"I know!" he said.

Chapter Eleven

The Frenzy

Hunting the fox has never been my kind of thing. Foxes may dish out some pretty smelly crap and make a mess of the odd bin bag left out overnight, but I retain a high regard for these skinny, ginger corgis. All the more so now that I have experienced what it feels like for the poor bloody fox when he's 'gone to earth'. This phrase describes the moment when a fox seeks to avoid the baying pack by diving down a hole in the ground. It is regarded as somewhat unsporting. The hounds are too big to follow, so they just mill about around the entrance - howling, sniffing, yawning and pissing. At some point the fox will have to come out and the fun begins all over again. The hunters usually pop a couple of terriers down the hole to have a quiet word with this scared, skulking, sulking wild animal and persuade it to rejoin the game.

Jamie and me, safe for a night or two in a ward at the Blue Mountain District Anzac Memorial Hospital. Outside the hospital entrance, about two hundred press and TV folk strung about with cameras, microphone booms and associated paraphernalia just hanging around for the long wait, occasionally attempting to sniff out a bit of copy to pad out their end product.

The doors that led out to this shanty town of international media folk were flanked by stone panels upon which were carved the names of New South Walers fallen in the service of Empire - Gallipoli, Palestine, Flanders, Singapore, Tobruk and elsewhere. The hospital had been erected as a memorial to those glorious dead, lain down in some corner of a foreign field that remains forever Australia. I felt the dignity of this entrance to be somewhat sullied by the gaudy throng milling around outside it.

The hospital manageress, Andrea Williams, insists that the hospital must always be referred to by its full name - not the Katoomba Hospital, not even the Blue Mountain Hospital - but the Blue Mountain District ANZAC Memorial Hospital. She dreads the arrival of outraged correspondence from veterans, and those who keep faith with them, if anyone dares to abbreviate the name by failing to include that emotive 'ANZAC'. This acronym, for Australian New Zealand Army Corps, has a resonance in the land of Australia that trumps anything as trivial as my own buffoonery on a plaza outside those doors, dedicated to the memory of fallen heroes. The name of the hospital is therefore a six word mouthful and it is by no means easy, under the stress of interview, to remember those words in the right order. I tried my best and though I got many things wrong in the days that followed, at least *The Mail on Sunday* got it right when I gave them my time the following week.

We were foxes in a hole. The media pack a-baying at the door had even set up cameras on the grassy knoll outside our first floor window. While Jamie lay abed, I was obliged to crawl on my hands and knees beneath the level of the windows to fetch something from my bag. Jamie was recovering well from his ordeal and by the following afternoon, Friday the 17th July, we would have to run for it. The Blue Mountain District ANZAC Memorial Hospital is not a hotel. If you're well enough to go home, you gotta be on your way.

The two days and nights I spent with Jamie in that ward are among the sweetest memories of the entire episode of Jamie's disappearance and return. The hospital staff were unfailingly kind and helpful, without bothering us unnecessarily. There were male and female nurses, dinner staff and security guards - dignified, hard-working men and women quietly carrying on with their work. No one offered them great wads of money for their trouble. Jamie and I watched a bit of TV, flicking between the channels to catch the news. I talked about things I once thought I would never get the chance to talk about, including that botched rendezvous at Krispy Kreme in Sydney. Jamie was still down in the mouth, touchy at times. It was not easy to tell if he was feeling sorry for himself or embarrassed about the fuss he'd engendered. Things had changed so much from misery to joy in so short a time that it was hard for me to take it in, let alone my son. There's the bit in 'Ben Hur' where Charlton Heston goes from galley slave to become the protégé of Jack Hawkins, with slave girls dancing and music playing and guys in leopard skin nappies tossing rose petals around the place and they're just lounging about, chilling out together. I had my boy back. It was like getting my own life back. I had thought my life was going to be nothing but utter misery till the day I die, dealing with Jean's anguish while struggling with my own feelings of rage and sorrow. Now things would be fine.

Andrea strongly advised us to get a media agent. She was a good friend in our hour of need and did a brilliant job of protecting her patient from the mob battering at the gates, but she clearly found dancing attention upon a media supernova something of a drain upon her time and energy. She had a whole hospital to run and my boy was not the only patient, not even the only one on the ward. She was spending too much of her time dealing with the security necessary to keep the press at bay whilst allowing access for legitimate patients, staff and visitors. Whenever she dropped by, she would hand over wads of notes, some in envelopes, some not, some printed and some just scribbled on torn notepaper, begging letters from journos - "phone me, speak to me, do a deal with us, we can look after you, tell us what you want". Then there were other well-wishers. Churches that had earnestly prayed for my son now sent cards articulating thanks to God, or Our Lady, eager to share their joy with the object of those bountifully answered prayers. An anonymous bushwalker, turned sadly away at the door, left him her whistle as a gift. Good people. I encouraged Jamie to hang onto these disinterested expressions of relief at his return. When he had time, he must write and thank them all for their kindness to a stranger in their midst.

Jamie was particularly delighted with the gift of a flower arrangement from a local florist. The flowers were a striking mix of pink, orange and yellow banksias. The flower heads were huge spiky balloons, vaguely reminiscent of cacti - unmistakably Australian. It crossed my mind that 'Katoomba Florists' might be the same place that Jeff had bought the roses. I phoned him up in Perth. He described the location of the shop he'd got them from. There were two florists in the main street of Katoomba. He had bought our roses from the one furthest from the railway. I phoned up 'Katoomba Florists' and asked them which one of the two they were. Sad to say, it was not the one that had supplied the roses. When we eventually made a run for it, at Jamie's insistence, those banksias came too.

All this attention was hardly conducive to the smooth running of the hospital. There were other issues on Andrea's workload, more mundane perhaps, but infinitely more relevant to the rest of the patients who attended the place. An agent would take some of this workload off her shoulders and the agent could arrange our exit from the hospital. There was quite simply no way we could walk out by ourselves, stroll down the main street to the Youth Hostel and book a room for the night with two hundred over-excited pressmen and women soliciting attention at every step. Without an agent we were unlikely to be welcome. No inexpensive hotel or hostel could provide a refuge for us. Who would pay for security staff? What about the other guests? Celebrity shares much in common with leprosy.

Some people find this agent business contemptible - the point when a young man's moving tale of grit descends to the grubby pursuit of money,

money, money. They should try leading an ordinary life whilst buffeted by a media scrum.

There were a couple of other reasons why we needed an agent, apart from the good of the hospital and the need for support when we hit the road. I was determined to put on a party for the Search and Rescue staff and this was not easy to arrange while we were under siege and had no access to internet. One of the senior police officers who came to see the boy suggested Gearin's hotel as the ideal place to go, whilst simultaneously stressing that none of his officers would be permitted to attend.

"I may stop briefly by for a soda water".

The New South Wales Police Service could not be seen to be accepting a reward for duty well done and, in particular, any suggestion that his officers might be accepting liquor at the expense of a private individual such as me was out of the question. I did not realise it at the time, but Jeff and I had already knocked back a couple of beers at Gearin's the previous Saturday. I had spent much of the time running to the gents' toilet to purge the liquefied remnants of a barramundi fish from my bottom.

It was a rough, tough, blue-collar drinking hole, with live music and several bars. As I sat straining on the toilet pan, I eavesdropped on f-word interspersed assertions from blokes who urinated against the wall outside my cubicle. It was not *The Carrington*.

I was told that the place was owned by Jack Thompson, the well-known Australian actor. Never heard of him.

If we did a deal with an interested news organisation, we could ask them to finance the party in exchange for coverage. But time was short. I was booked to fly home on Saturday afternoon, so the only available night would be Friday. We were expecting to leave the hospital on the afternoon of that day.

Then, of course, there was the money. I had given away interviews to channels Nine and Seven on Wednesday morning and given the rest of the pack good copy of a delighted buffoon turning metaphorical cartwheels in celebration of the boy being back in town. I was genuinely concerned to give something back to this wonderful community - particularly the guys and sheilas who had been literally beating around the bush for day after day, come rain and shine, until some of them literally collapsed from exhaustion. If people were keen to pay for my very own musings upon the latter day Lazarus, I was equally keen to grab that cash and pass it on to the Search and Rescue folk. It was not easy. Like the police, the Search and Rescue Service (SRS) is careful to avoid accepting gifts for doing their duty. Any contribution had to arrive through 'official channels'. In other words, we could send cheques to the British High Commission and they would make an equivalent donation to the SRS. Another possible avenue whereby I could pay back whatever I was paid was by means of a donation to the Blue Mountains District ANZAC Memorial Hospital.

I had been recorded on camera, stating that I wanted nothing for myself out of this wonderful event and I am not one to go back on my word. I detest those who can't keep their promises. The motto of the City of London financial community is 'verbum est pactum' - 'my word is my bond'. It's also mine. Unlike the spivs of the City, I meant every word. Getting my son back was treasure enough for me. It was not something I had discussed with my son before the question about money was thrown at me. I answered, characteristically, off the cuff.

Jamie was a bit embarrassed by this approach. He recognised the debt he owed to the hospital and the SRS and was happy to make a substantial donation to those agencies in partial discharge of that debt. He was also intending to go to Exeter University when he got back home. Before he went away to Oz he had talked about borrowing some money to buy a flat while he was a student. He was hopelessly optimistic. Who would be crazy enough to lend him enough cash to buy rather than rent while he was still a student?

"Your mate Michael, maybe?"

The prospect of Jamie touting for loans from my better off friends was not one I welcomed. Now he stood to earn a lot of money. Maybe now that flat was not so far out of reach. I had no problem with all this. I was fortunate to have a job and a mortgage that was manageable at a time of life when my children were almost ready to join the world of work and pay-your-own-way. A real estate investment at the age of nineteen would provide a good launch pad for his future prospects. I felt I had only committed myself to the policy of non-profitability. My son's stupidity should be a source of shame to me, not profit. Jamie is legally an adult and must do what he feels is comfortable for him. I never held myself out as his spokesman. I spoke for myself. Some newspapers assumed I spoke for both of us.

The issue of whether Aussie tax-payers should pour forth their tax-dollars time and time again, plucking lost hikers from the consequences of their failure to follow paths, tell others where they're off to, take enough food and water etc., was a very live issue in the days that followed Jamie's reappearance. The fact that too many of these lost bushwalkers were not themselves Australian tax-payers but foreign tourists and, more often than not, bloody Poms was not lost on the not-for-profit faction and lent a nationalistic edge to the debate. The 2009 Ashes test series was actually in progress while we stayed in the hospital, crowned by victory for the home nation in the second test at Lords. The view was not necessarily that of a majority. There are plenty of Australians who argue that human life is far too important to price up and that, as the Search and Rescue Service is up, running and paid for even when no one is actually missing, the extra cost incurred by a genuine emergency, as opposed to, say, a training exercise, is not so great. The prospect of some blubbing tourist, albeit possibly a Pom, being choppered away from some remote outcrop only after he hands over his credit card details to the bloke on the end of the rope is not one most Aussies could live with. They are a fundamentally generous, warm-hearted people, with a sense of social responsibility and community networking that is no longer so pronounced in most parts of Great Britain. I was shortly to meet one of the few Australians who did not measure up to this ideal.

My high-minded attitude to payback was a genuine point of principle, but I also recognised that there was a substantial body of opinion that viewed Jamie's return from the Valley of the Shadow of Death as hoax rather than miracle. I will have a good deal to say in rebuttal of this nonsense in due course but, for the moment, I only state that I recognised the presence and strength of this undercurrent and felt that by far the best way to deal with it was to stress our lack of obvious avarice. I was mindful that Jamie might find himself in a dangerous situation if he met up with some grizzled ex-searcher aggrieved by the notion that while he, the searcher, had been sweating through the bush, Jamie had sat it out in a cave full of Mars bars waiting for the right moment to resurface. The fact is that it would have taken the foresight of Nostradamus to have anticipated the global newsworthiness of the Jamie Neale resurrection. Teenagers go missing every day. Some turn up - dead or alive. Some don't. Most don't even make their local paper. I am still not sure about what is was that turned this particular disappearance and reappearance into worldwide news, but have no doubt that his twelve day ordeal and my own nine day anguish were absolutely genuine.

Chapter Twelve

The Deal

Andrea had been in touch with the person responsible for media management on behalf of New South Wales Health Service. She produced an e-mail with the names of two Sydney based publicists. Jamie was not keen. I stressed how important it was to get something in place to arrange our exit from the hospital. We received these two names at midday on Wednesday. Jamie was due to be discharged on the Friday. I was flying out on Saturday afternoon and we needed to sort out a party for the Search and Rescue people. The only suitable date for a party would be Friday evening. Time was very short. We still needed to arrange the venue and make sure people got their invitation to come.

Jamie was still morose and I had to work hard to get him to cooperate. I felt we had to do a deal with a publicist and do it quickly. The party was important to me - a debt of honour. I had said we would party and was worried about losing my credibility if we failed to deliver. It was also something I looked forward to for my own selfish pleasure; a celebration of Jamie's return, a chance for me to have a drink and a dance and a generally good time with a great bunch of guys and gals. I needed it. I may even have thought I deserved it after the strain I'd been through. I told Jamie that I understood his misgivings but the expectations of the searchers were more important. They had to be thanked for all their effort on his behalf.

Jamie later resented the way I railroaded the deal through, but I thought we had little alternative in the limited time available. He was to accuse me of 'bouncing' him into the arrangement. I am not sure how things would have worked out if Jamie had been on his own. There would probably been a party, but at a later date. I have no idea what he would have done about exiting the hospital with no car or place to go and two hundred press people running in pursuit. I later had reasons to regret the deal and I know that the resentment engendered by Jamie's feeling that I had rushed him into something against his will was a factor in the rift that developed between us. The best of motives sowed the worst of consequences. It's the Australian way.

We tossed a coin to decide which of the two agents we would contact. The name that won the toss was Sean Anderson. And so it came about that a serpent did enter upon my paradise. Maybe there's a parallel universe where the coin comes up tails and we get the guy called Macnamara instead. I get paid for my interviews, make the donations and get a gong for services to Anglo-Australian concord. My son and I live in relative harmony.

What we ought to have done was contact both agents and each of us choose one. The idea that there could be a conflict of interest between me and Jamie simply did not occur to me. No doubt there are plenty of readers who are outraged that we should require any agent at all, let alone two. We were in a situation where literally hundreds of media outlets wanted their piece of this story. We were in no position ourselves to negotiate with any of them. I was committed to the position that I was happy to accept the dollar bills on offer, but I would be remitting them to the 'good causes' - the agencies who had worked so hard to find Jamie and care for him after he was found. The alternative idea that we could have simply walked away - no publicity agent, no big money deals - is simply unrealistic. We had nowhere to go. We would be pursued and hassled and badgered and photographed wherever we tried to hide. The media would get their story for free - probably a shot of Cass lashing out at a cameraman. The good causes would get nothing. A good agent would sell our stories for what they were worth to the media. The SRS and the Blue Mountain District ANZAC Memorial Hospital would be the winners. That was the best plan, so far as I was concerned.

We told hospital security that Sean Anderson was permitted inside our security cordon. I must pay tribute to the guys who maintained this cordon. We heard about the many ruses that enterprising newsmen and women use to get those saleable shots of 'celebrities' in hospitals and such like. These include such stratagems as dressing up as medics or claiming to be visiting relatives in the same part of the hospital. Jamie got visits from all the people he wanted to see, including the couple who found him, and no one got into the ward that shouldn't have done. This was a busy hospital with plenty of other patients, including some who shared the same ward. The security guys were big, bald, tough looking men. They did a fantastic job in very difficult circumstances.

Sean had to drive up from Sydney, so it was mid-afternoon when he arrived on the ward. He was a slim, slick-looking thirty-something - cropped hair and steel-rimmed spectacles. With his razored scalp, tall skinny frame and piano keyboard teeth, he instantly recalled 'Plug' – from *'The Bash Street Kids'* in the *'Beano'*. He wore a pale fawn-coloured suit. In a surprisingly deep, arrogant voice he told us that he would require twenty-five per cent of any deal he was able to negotiate on our behalf. Our jaws dropped. We were naive about these things but not that naive.

"That sounds a lot". I said. He was assuming we were idiots.

"Well, that's the industry standard, I'm afraid. You have to pay for the best. I represented the Beaconsfield Miners".

We had not heard of the Beaconsfield Miners. We would be hearing a great deal about them in the two days to come.

Jamie asked if Sean could leave us alone to discuss his proposal. Sean left the room.

"I don't like him. I think we should say 'no'".

I didn't like the guy either, but it was half past two and we had a party to sort out. If we phoned the other agent on the list, it would be five o'clock at the earliest before he reached us. What would happen if the other guy was equally naff? Twenty-five per cent was way over the top. Despite the way he had got our backs up, I felt some responsibility for calling Sean out on a fool's errand. I should have asked what percentage he charged when I first spoke to him by phone. He had driven eighty kilometres to hear that his pug-ugly, Plug-ugly face didn't fit.

At this point, Jamie was called away for some medical procedure. I was left to break the news to Sean. The room we occupied was a kitchenette for the convenience of hospital staff with instant coffee, milk in the fridge, water boiler and a sink. Every so often a nurse would pop in and out. They mostly apologised and left us to our meeting.

"Sorry, Sean. We're not happy with you". I began.

As a face at first just pasty turned a paler shade of pink.

"What's the problem?"

I should have said, "Sorry, but you're just not right for us", and walked away. Not for the first time in my life, common decency led me to perdition. The fatal flaw of preferring compromise to conflict sapped my resolution.

"Twenty-five per cent is far too much".

"I can go down to twenty per cent".

Jamie returned, expecting me to have sent Sean on his way. I told him Sean had dropped his percentage to twenty. The unspoken question between us was "Do we still say 'no'?".

"Can you go down to seventeen and a half?" said Jamie.

I was impressed that he had the confidence to haggle and grateful that we were not dismissing the guy and heading back to square one.

"Done!"

We shook hands on the deal; without enthusiasm on our side, no doubt with considerable relief on Sear s. We should have run down the bastard down to twelve and a half. Much, much better still - booted him out on his scrawny backside!

He produced two contracts to sign. There were no copies for us. Maybe it had not occurred to him that he would be signing up the two of us. We had to insist on getting copies as soon as possible. He told us the Jamie Neale story could be worth at least half a million dollars. We had done the right thing, he assured us. I attempted to discuss my wish that the Sydney *'Daily Telegraph'* should be given special consideration on account of the positive coverage they had provided over the past week or so. They had kept Jamie's plight in the public mind and this must have helped encourage the fantastic response from the search volunteers which I had witnessed out on the trail. I had also spoken to the London *'Daily Telegraph'* in response to one of the many bits of scribbled notepaper handed to me on my brief appearances outside. I knew this was my mum's favourite read. The London guys had told me they were not in the business of paying out massive fees for news stories but they were sympathetic to my suggestion about paying for four trail bikes to donate to the Rescue Service. When I was outside, holding forth to Channel Nine and Channel Seven at six o'clock that morning, a couple of quietly spoken young men had approached me. They were conspicuous by their edgy, ungroomed appearance and their lack of microphones and trailing cables. They said they had been riding the paths on trail bikes for the Rescue Service in the search for Jamie. They claimed they could have done more, but had been hampered by the small size of their petrol tanks I said that if there was anything I could do to help sort that out, I would do it. I shook their hands and thanked them for their efforts to find my son. Then they were swept aside by that pushing, pleading, elbowing, interrupting goose gaggle of media folk. I stepped back into the enchanted circle of the hospital building, where big, bald men in leather jackets kept mayhem at bay. God bless 'em.

The eyes behind Sean's spectacles showed no enthusiasm for this kind of nonsense, nor did my insistence that I was not out to make money for myself generate any response from him. I suspect he was focused on Jamie. This old man was a sort of add-on who could be tolerated as long as he didn't rock the boat. He did not see me as any kind of threat to his hold over Jamie's earning potential, nor someone whose wishes might need to be taken into consideration. Nor would I have seen myself in such a light. I was reasonably content - much more so than Jamie.

Sean asked us if there was anything we needed. We were trapped in the ward. It was not as if we could casually pop out for a packet of biscuits. We could not even visit the hospital shop. I tried once and met up with that same long-haired roadie reporter who had shadowed me since my arrival in Katoomba. This corridor encounter occurred shortly after I'd signed up with Sean, so, even now, the poor bloke lost out. I hope Roadie's bosses read this one day and realise how hard the poor guy tried to get my story.

We both needed socks and I needed an adapter to charge up my phone. Jamie held up tattered and mud stained trainers.

"Size eleven".

He needed shirt and trousers too. At this stage he was dressed in the pale blue hospital pajamas. The clothes he had left at the hostel were still with the police and the clothes he had worn in the forest were, of course, indescribably foul and unfit to wear. He had used his torn off shirt sleeves as socks.

"I need to find a hotel and set up an office," said Sean. He said he would be back later with copies of the contract and the trainers, socks, shirt etc.

Jamie remained moody. "You bounced me into that".

I explained once again how important it was to me to do the deal for the sake of the party at Gearin's. We had yet to find out if Gearin's could accommodate the party at such short notice. Jamie revisited this issue several times over the next couple of days. I was patient with him because I realised that he was still psychologically fragile after what he had been through. Inwardly I thought he was being a pain about it. This was a chance to give something back to the guys and girls who had suffered in the search for him. Jamie felt the debt he owed to these people, but was unhappy that I had rushed him into a deal he was not ready for. He brooded on it and resented my own insistence that, while I claimed to understand his feelings, I still felt I had done the right thing. I dare say my own ebullient spirits must have grated on his own more subdued reaction to his survival. Nothing annoys the miserable more than the joy of those in their proximity. When I came to fall out with Sean, Jamie could reasonably point out that I was the one who had insisted on first getting involved with the ratbag.

While Sean was out shopping, Jamie was well enough to sit through two hours of debriefing by New South Wales Police. They were able to satisfy themselves about where he had been lost, mainly because he had encountered a bats' roost. There was only one significant bats' roost in the valley. He had also seen a feral horse. I asked why he hadn't jumped on its back and trotted back to Katoomba.

Jamie was not the only patient on the ward. We spent a bit of our time chatting to the elderly Yorkshireman who came in with angina. We shared memories of the city of Leeds. He had emigrated away from there in the sixties, fifteen years before I commenced my degree at Leeds University. It was a delight to hear the dour diction of the North again, in a place so remote from the old country.

Later that evening, Sean came back with the clothes. Jamie was impressed with the trainers. They were expensive. Sean had made sure the price tag was still attached. He had been in contact with various interested parties, but nothing had been finalised. I suggested Sean and I could pop down to Gearin's hotel to sort out the arrangements for the party. Sean was okay with this. I looked forward to getting out of the hospital, even if only for an hour or so.

Most of the camera crews had given up for the night as we made our way to Sean's black Range Rover, but we still found ourselves trailed all the way to Gearin's by a couple of the more persistent crews.

We found the joint without any problems and went inside to order a beer. Sean Anderson was still immaculately attired in his fawn-coloured suit and looked out of place in this blue collar drinking den. He was probably the only bloke in a suit who drank there that month. With my untidy beard and belted denims, I must have blended in well. We looked an odd couple to be out drinking together. A slightly tipsy woman approached to congratulate me on getting my son back. I said thank you. We hugged.

Sean asked the bartender if we could speak to the manager. The manager turned out to be another Sean. Sean Anderson introduced himself and introduced me as the father of the lad who had been lost down in the valley. I explained that Gearin's had been recommended as a good place to celebrate getting the boy back. Gearin's Sean was laconically agreeable. He took us upstairs to show us a couple of function rooms. We chose the one we were most happy with. We pointed out that we would need decent security to keep the press at bay. How much was it all going to cost?

"You can have it on us".

Sounded dead decent of him. Maybe we wouldn't be needing a media sponsor to pick up the bill after all.

Sean dropped me off outside the hospital. I found Jamie in bed with the remains of a pizza. A local pizza company had sent in some of their pizza as a kind of thank you for him getting stuffed with pizza on the night before he went walkabout. It had been wonderful advertisement for the nutritional value of pizza, particularly for anyone thinking of skipping a decent meal for the best part of a fortnight.

I felt happy. I'd got Jamie back. We'd got the party sorted and Jamie seemed a lot happier too.

I bedded down for my second night on the camp bed beside my son.

Chapter Thirteen

The Party

Next morning Sean was back. He had duplicated copies of the contract. The good news was that he had arranged a deal with Channel Nine's *'Sixty Minutes'* program. It was a good deal for the Search and Rescue Service as well as Jamie. Jamie had asked Sean to be sensitive to the issue surrounding media payments by getting something for the SRS out of any financial arrangement. Like every other concession to tender conscience in the land that invented the boomerang, Jamie's best intentions went on to generate worse headlines than if we had behaved like complete carpet baggers. The deal was flagged up as being worth $200,000. Half that figure was a gift of TV advertising time for the SRS to promote their bushwalking beacons. A lot of people got it into their heads that Jamie got paid the whole amount and then failed to honour 'a promise' to give half of it in cash to the SRS.

At one point, Sean and Jamie had a private discussion in the kitchenette. I thought nothing of this.

The money was good, but I was still committed to donating my share to the good causes. Jamie also spoke about generous donations to the hospital and SRS. I was pleased he was mindful of the debt he owed to these organisations. He would not be giving all his media earnings away. He had not committed himself in the way I had and it was understandable that a young man in his position would welcome the opportunity to make some money. He was about to go off to university and may well have felt his suffering and survival entitled him to some recompense. After Sean had gone, I thought it was a good idea to discuss the way we would be dealing with the money we earned from media appearances in order to avoid the potential for any misunderstanding or resentment. I suggested we should be paid individually for each thing we do on our own. How were we splitting the payments on things we did together? I was not only talking in terms of the *'Sixty Minutes'* program. I was flying back to the UK the next day. I wanted to know what would happen to any money I made over there. I was later to be accused of demanding 'half' Jamie's money. There was no such demand. I was inviting Jamie to enter an amicable negotiation. I saw the *'Sixty Minutes'* program in terms of separate individual interviews for father and son, with separate fees to be agreed by our agent, Sean Anderson. I was well aware that the fee for Jamie's participation would be substantially greater than mine. The scenes we did together could be split 50/50 or 20/80 or however the parties decided. In the unlikely event that there was a deadlock, Sean would be in a position to arbitrate on the basis of his media savvy assessment of what our respective appearances were worth.

I have no doubt that this cold blooded capitulation of my thoughts on how we ought to distribute the media payments flowing from Jamie's ordeal will seem grubby and even greedy to many people. It was not. I was interested in making money not for myself, but for the SRS and the hospital. I wanted to pay Australia back for their generosity to my son in his hour of need. Jamie was also keen to pay substantial sums of money to the same good causes. I therefore believed that it was important to discuss the distribution of the money in order to make sure we were on a similar wavelength, rather than making assumptions about each other's position which might lead to problems in the future. This is, of course, precisely what did happen. At that stage, I certainly did not see any reason why we should fall out over this. It was sensible to sort these things out at an early stage but I was already too late. Sean and Jamie had sorted it out between them, without involving me.

There was to be no negotiation. It mattered not a jot what I thought.

"You said you didn't want anything".

I had not said anything of the sort. I wanted to make some money, so that I could fulfill what I'd said in front of the world about giving it back to Australia.

It was a *fait accompli*. Jamie would get the money minus Sean's commission. I would get nothing. I was not happy, but I had to bite my tongue. We were in a hospital and my son was a patient. I didn't want a row about it when there was so much to do. I felt sure that once Jamie had thought about it he would realise he was being unreasonable. He was getting his own back for my 'bouncing' him into the agreement with Sean.

I later found out that there was another reason why he was unhappy with me. He mistakenly believed that I had put the phone down on his mother during a phone call on Wednesday. He did not mention this to me until much later. If he had done so I would have explained that I had done nothing of the sort. My battery had simply run out of charge.

Perhaps I should have declined to cooperate with the *'Sixty Minutes'* team unless or until I got a promise of payment. It was not that easy to walk away. I wanted to remain with Jamie after we exited the hospital. I had nowhere else to go. Nor did I wish to make a scene. I did not even know if they wanted a piece of me or if they were only talking to Jamie. The situation was not of Channel Nine's making. They had made the deal with Sean in good faith. Why should I play awkward, especially as they were laying on a helicopter to get me to Sydney Airport after my own interview? I was also very grateful to Channel Nine for the chopper ride I got on the day I reached Katoomba. I knew that Jamie was more important to them than me. It would be unseemly for me to try to 'bounce' the issue, when they were paying a lot of money and working to a tight time frame. I went with the flow. Had I not attempted to raise the issue with Jamie, he probably would have left me in ignorance of the fact I was not being paid for my part in the documentary until I was out of the country. By happenstance or design, Jamie and I were kept apart for most of the time we were with the Channel Nine crew.

I have gone into this matter in tedious and distasteful detail because inaccurate reports of what was 'agreed' and equally inaccurate reports of what I 'demanded' were to be bandied about in the weeks to come. The first important thing to say is that there was no agreement of any kind. Jamie did not 'go back on an agreement' to split all the cash in half. I only wanted payment for what I did, stressing once more that I was not collecting anything for myself. There was no 'agreement' because there was nothing to agree about. The deal had been done. All the money was going to Jamie. It had been decided between Jamie and Sean, without reference to me. Nor did I renege on 'an agreement' to accept payment for flights and the Gearin's bar tab in settlement of this issue. Jamie certainly did, at a later time, offer to pay these expenses but an offer is not an agreement. It was my choice to fly to Australia. I did not expect anyone else to pay for it. The bar tab should have been paid by Channel Nine. As they failed to do so, I am ruefully content to have treated those rescue guys and gals to a drink at my expense. This lapse on the part of Channel Nine had nothing to do with Jamie. I don't want Jamie or anyone else to pay my expenses. I acknowledge that I did receive some help from mum and some money collected by my work colleagues. The latter had to hand it to me in a disguised package. Expenses had nothing to do with the issue of payment for services rendered by me in connection with an agreement negotiated by an agent contractually acting on my behalf. At the time that Jamie offered to pay these costs, I did not understand that he intended me to connect the two. I believed I was entitled to get paid for the interview and the commitment to exclusivity which Sean agreed with Channel Nine as my appointed agent. Why should they get this for nothing at a time when there were plenty of other news organisations offering silly money for my story? I owed it to the rescuers to get as much for it as I could, so I could pay them back. The ugliest canard I had to endure in the following weeks was that I had asked for half of Jamie's money. I neither asked for nor wanted any of Jamie's money. That does not mean I wanted nothing for selling my own story. Nor does it mean I wanted Jamie to get paid for my story. Thus did wormwood curdle the ambrosia of my son's return.

I sometimes wonder what induced Sean to collude with Jamie in depriving me of any payment for taking part in the *'Sixty Minutes'* documentary. He later took the position that Jamie had told him I didn't want to be paid and it was therefore a matter between me and my son. This is an outrageous escape clause. He had ample opportunity to talk to me directly about my wishes. I had certainly not indicated that my son had been delegated to speak on my behalf. Why on earth had I signed Sean up as my agent if I did not expect him to protect my financial interest in any sale of my story? It does not take a genius to work out that negotiating a deal on behalf of two clients whereby one gets paid and the other doesn't was bound to cause ill feeling. The fact I was going to give the money away does not mean I did not feel aggrieved at not getting it in the first place. I am convinced that if Sean had taken the trouble to negotiate separate payments for Jamie and me, the two of us would be on amicable terms to this day. We certainly would have had our differences, but it was the public perception that one or both of us were 'arguing about money' that sickened the public and drove us apart. According to his company website, Sean trained as a lawyer. He must therefore be aware of the rules governing conflicts of interest in a legal context. I would have been more impressed with Sean if he had ceased to blather about his labours on behalf of the Beaconsfield Miners and insisted that he could not, in good conscience, represent both of us and therefore advised one or other of us to find alternative representation. It may be that Sean regarded Jamie as the Jewel in his Crown. I might be dissatisfied with these inequitable arrangements but it was not in my interest to make a fuss.

Jamie was the one who mattered. I was going to have to lump it. If Sean did think that, then he was right. That is what I did. It was not this petty dispute about money that caused me to 'flip'.

Jamie was due to be discharged on Friday afternoon. He had made a good recovery from his ordeal, though he still had emphysema; that is to say, air bubbles within his chest cavity. He was advised that these would probably disperse without any problems but they could be dangerous in conditions of low atmospheric pressure. He was strongly advised not to fly. The doctor had arranged an appointment with a specialist for the following fortnight. If that went well, he might be cleared to fly. Jamie was keen to spend more time with his Uncle Jeff in Western Australia as soon as he had finished his commitments in New South Wales. At the time I left him, I assumed that he would travel by train rather than plane. In the event, the check-up by the specialist went well and he was able to fly back across the continent. I feel he missed out on the experience of a lifetime by not taking the train across the Nullarbor. If he had gone down that route, he would have the pleasure of knowing that he had travelled as far across the surface of the planet in a straight line (though obviously in a curve round the spherical shape of the earth) as it is possible to do on a choo-choo.

Channel Nine had booked us into a hotel at a secret location. Along with Sean, they would choreograph our exit from the hospital. They also wanted the right to film an interview with Jamie from his hospital bed just before he was discharged and they had arranged for one of the hospital doctors to conduct an examination of the patient on camera.

The camera crew appeared around lunchtime. They introduced themselves and explained what they intended to do. Andrea arrived with a message that a straggler was trying to rejoin them after getting separated outside the hospital.

"That old trick!" they laughed. I was never able to work out whether they were having a laugh at the expense of a hapless and genuinely lost crew member or whether there really had been an attempt to breach the security cordon by subterfuge. There exists an intense rivalry between the various TV crews. They love to obstruct each other and interrupt the others' interviews or even detain and distract a person of interest simply to frustrate a rival.

The crew consisted of Nick, Alexander, Bruce and a couple of others. The presenter was yet another media blonde, Tara Brown.

She interviewed Jamie while he sat by his bed. I wasn't needed. I sat at the far end of the room. Jamie coped well with the interview. He came across as a serious, thoughtful and contrite young man. At one point he was asked to show his mucky clothes to the camera, the clothes he had worn throughout his twelve days in the bush. The smell alone would have sufficed to convince any doubters that this was not a stunt. Unfortunately, although the word 'Smellivision' has been coined in anticipation thereof, TV technology is not yet able to record or transmit olfactory sense data. The smell had been a problem for Jamie himself when he tried to wrap his head in the shirt to conserve body heat on the cold nights in the bush. He had alternated that unbearable stench with bone chilling cold. He showed how he had ripped the sleeves off his shirt so he could use them as socks.

When the doctor arrived I did not realise that he had come to examine my son on camera. I expected him to shoo the cameras away so he could conduct vital medical procedures undistracted by the trivialities of this media freak show. In fact, he was eager to show off his medical expertise on TV and had apparently rearranged his schedule to suit the convenience of the crew. He was happy to state on camera that Jamie's health was consistent with his having been living out in the wild for twelve days.

Breakout was scheduled for four o'clock.

We packed our bags and said our goodbyes to the staff who had been so kind to us, then it was off down the corridor at a brisk marching pace. The posse included the guys from Channel Nine, along with Andrea and the security staff. As we came through the doors into the fading daylight, it was as if a firework party had exploded into life. Sean had told us to say nothing to the press pack, except a few words of thanks from Jamie. This was easy for me as no one bothered about me. Jamie was at the centre of the scrum while I trailed behind. He was forced by the pressure to go round the car and enter through the door on the far side of Sean's black Range Rover. I had no trouble getting in on the near side. Then we were off, with the press pack in full cry. Sean drove fast and furiously to shake off the convoy behind us, then it was up the slope to those grand stone stairs leading up to the swanky *Carrington Hotel*. This was a bluff. We had to run right through the hotel and jump into a second vehicle waiting on a service road out back, driven by Nick. Sean stayed behind to collect his own car. It was exciting, cloak and dagger stuff, the adrenaline pounding through our blood.

The ruse succeeded in shaking off the press gang. We drove through Katoomba with our heads down and out towards Leura.

We then got lost for a time in the back roads of Leura. Nick turned round to ask Jamie if he wanted a meal waiting for him when we got to our hotel. Jamie asked for steak and chips. Nick immediately got on the phone to make the order. I assumed he would turn back to me and ask if I wanted anything. He didn't. Jamie was as flabbergasted as me by the discourtesy. We stared at one another wide eyed that anyone could be so rude as to feed the son but ignore the equally famished father sitting alongside him.

I don't think Nick intended to snub me. He had a tendency to focus his mind entirely on things he considered important, so as not to hear or even notice someone or something not in that category. Sean had a similar manner. It may be a personality trait of tall, successful thirty-something alpha males, heartily resented by the gammas and deltas of the gene pool.

Rather than be obliged to share remnants of my son's medium rare steak, I interrupted Nick's phone conversation.

"Is it okay if I have something to eat too?"

"Oh yeah, sorry".

I asked for a burger.

Leura is a town a few miles east of Katoomba. It is smaller and, if it's possible, quieter than its neighbour. We had been booked in to the *Leura Fairmont Hotel*. This is a large and luxurious establishment set in its own extensive grounds. The schedule was very tight. They wanted to film another interview with Jamie at a studio that had been set up in one of the hotel rooms. Then we had to head back to Katoomba for the Search and Rescue Party at eight. Early the following morning, they wanted to take Jamie out along the track to Ruined Castle, then they wanted to do an interview with me and set up a farewell scene. I would then be driven to a local airfield and catch the Channel Nine chopper to take me to Sydney where I would board my three pm flight back to Blighty.

Jamie's interview at the hotel recapitulated the matters that had been discussed at the bedside interview a few hours earlier, but then the questions seemed to move into more personal and probing territory. What was Jamie's state of mind as he endured day after day of frustration and want? Jamie talked of his fear of starvation and how much he missed his family. He talked about how much he loved his mum and how much she was on his mind when he worried he might never see her again. Tara asked the obvious continuation. "How about your dad?"

The reply was painfully dismissive. Tara was probably expecting a platitudinous tribute to the dad who'd dropped everything to come and find him.

"Yeah. I was a bit surprised to find he'd come over".

Thank you, my dear boy, for that ringing endorsement of my never-failing love for you.

This was not the unthinking lack of appreciation that most parents ruefully endure from time to time. Jamie was winding me up and he knew it. My consciousness exploded to that lonely wolf howl of the heart, the silent howl of every desperate, deadbeat dad who's ever juggled to do what's best for a son or daughter he loves so much, as the beloved brat simpers out cold calculation, "But Mummy always let us watch *'Chuckey's Revenge'*. You're just being mean!".

I did nothing heroic in boarding a plane to fly to Australia when I heard Jamie was in trouble. I am sure that ninety-nine per cent of parents would do the same, assuming that they had sufficient health and wealth to manage it. I cannot understand why Jamie wished to pigeonhole me with the one percent that didn't give a damn, except in terms of a deliberate slight. If Jamie genuinely found it so surprising that his father had cared enough to spend a week of time and a few thousand pounds of money to join in with the search for him, then he must have been living in a parallel universe to the son I'd seen grow up. Was he surprised that I had pulled him out of the Grand Union Canal rather than left him to drown? Was he surprised that I'd once grabbed a kitchen knife and gone out looking for the youths who had robbed him at knifepoint on his way home from school? I had given my children my every Sunday, attended their every school fete or parents' evening. Jamie was mad at me. I wasn't sure why. But he was playing with fire. I was near the end of twenty years of struggle to keep my children supplied with holidays, saxophone lessons, love and time. I loved my children. I was sorry I wasn't living with them. I was sorry they were not living with me. My relationship with them had defined my life since the time I took on responsibility for the lives I had brought into existence. Jamie was picking at raw and powerful emotions.

I do not know what demons drove my son to make light of my love and concern for him in front of a TV audience of millions, but it was another bone-scrunching thrust of the goad that would have me stampeding away by the end of the week. By that time, Jamie realised that he had gone too far. He was to issue a grudging apology and a promise not to say anything rotten about me again, but, by then, it was too late. I was too far gone to accept cynical apologies. I just carried on galloping towards the edge of the cliff. The interview was edited down. The comment was not even broadcast.

I had very little chance to talk to Jamie over the next twenty-four hours, but we did snatch a moment together in his hotel bedroom when we set down our bags. I complemented Jamie on how well he had coped with the interview. I told him I was unhappy about the way he had spoken about me. Predictably, Jamie complained of my having a go at him at such a stressful time. He offered to pay my travel expenses as a sop to my injured feelings. I was still on board the bus but I was sulking alone at the back.

We travelled separately to the Search and Rescue party, because Jamie had to do more filming. I would be holding the fort till he arrived. I was driven there by Nick, then ushered past the press pack and through the security cordon into a darkened room where the event was in swing. I had hoped there would be a band, but there was nothing to dance to, not even a DJ. The place was supposed to be a music venue. Was there no local rock band hungry for TV exposure? There was a buffet table and a free bar. The drinks were on the house or maybe on Channel Nine. I wasn't sure. But drink your fill, you lads and lasses. You've earned it. I had campaigned hard to drive this party into being. I was proud that we'd got something up and running at such short notice and under such curtailment of my freedom to get about.

I met quite a few of the great guys and ladies I'd seen out on the trail in very different circumstances. I met Becky for the first time, lovely, raven haired lass who had been in touch with Jean and Gary back in England. She asked me to deliver her best wishes to them when I got back. I was pleased to see Charlie Brown, one of the great characters of the rescue service, whom I had last seen at the top of the Golden Stairs. Now the worry and sheer physical effort was behind us. We were having a good time together. I was deeply touched by the modesty, warmth and dignity of all the people I met or re-met that night. The events of the last two weeks had meant a great deal to this Blue Mountain community. The awful dread of another tragedy had resolved into this happy ending and glad tidings all round the world. A couple of guys asked me to write messages on their copies of the eulogy

I'd written to my lost son, describing how special he was, how important it was to keep searching. Now they would be meeting the same remarkable young man in the flesh. I was presented with maps and a Rural Fire Service baseball cap by partygoersI circulated among the groups of drinkers, shaking hands with the men, hugging and kissing the ladies. I was having a great time. I posed for photos and drank my fill at the supposedly paid-for bar.

Jamie arrived after about half an hour and proceeded to do much the same as me, moving around the room introducing himself, thanking everyone for their hard work, sharing jokes and hugging ladies. He was given a Search and Rescue high-viz jacket to wear. We did not mingle much with each other, though I called him over once or twice to meet with revellers who had not yet had a chance to talk with him. I wanted to make sure everyone who had been out looking for him had their chance to speak with him. He needed to personally thank as many of these people as he could.

All the while the *'Sixty Minutes'* camera crew were following Jamie's progress, camera on Alex's shoulder, Bruce's boom maneuvering to catch the small talk. Jamie said how pleased he was that half the money from the TV deal was going to the SRS. This led to the misunderstanding about details of the deal that resulted in claims that he had promised half his earnings to the SRS.

This had all been going on for a while, when it was suggested that the pair of us should deliver our speeches of gratitude to the assembled throng. I had nothing prepared but I was very happy to go ahead. To cries of "Speech, speech!" the revellers were assembled in front of Jamie and me. Shortly before, I had been chatting to Doug, a big, bald man-mountain who had been one of the heroes of the search for Jamie Neale. He had wept tears of joy at being able to celebrate the happy ending with us at Gearin's. As I prepared to make my speech, he stood proudly alongside me, beer glass in hand. I had no problem with this. He was a mate of mine.

"Nah, get that guy out of the way!" ordered Nick.

The poor guy was unceremoniously bundled away.

"Hey! This is supposed to be about us," he snarled. 'We were the ones out looking for Jamie. Not you!"

Fair enough, I thought.

I was embarrassed by the sudden change in the atmosphere from a mood of celebration to one of confrontation. The camera crew were urban sophisticates choreographing tough, warm-hearted outdoorsmen and women. My loathing for Nick was ratcheted up a notch. The burger incident was a bit of farce. Shoving these guys around was not funny at all. I went up to Doug to apologise for the rough handling. When I eventually got to see the documentary that was put together by the *'Sixty Minutes'* crew, I was pleased to see that they had included footage of Doug speaking on camera, though not the earlier outburst. Maybe they thought they were making it up to him. I bloody well hope so.

In this slightly tense atmosphere, we delivered our respective speeches, thanked everyone for their generosity. Jamie apologised for getting so comprehensively lost in the first place and being so hard to find after he had done so.

I ended up enjoying myself too much to leave the party when the crew departed. I also felt I was a kind of host and had to hang on till the last guest had gone. Sean said he would come back later to pick me up.

By about eleven, most of the guests had gone on their way. I finished up back in the main bar, knocking back the beers with my new best buddy - 'Moose'. As the night wore on, I concluded that Sean had forgotten all about picking me up, so I was grateful when Moose made a 'Hey Honey, guess who I'm drinking with?' call to his missus to arrange a lift to take me back to the Fairmont. We were both at that happy stage of being slurred in speech and sentimental in our affections without yet becoming morose, obnoxious or aggressive.

At this point the other Sean, Gearin's manager Sean, rolled up with a scrap of paper for me. A$ 946.30, please.

"Er. This one's on us?"

"That was just the hire of the room. This is the bill for booze and security".

I gulped hard and handed over my credit card. I assumed I'd be getting the money back from Channel Nine in due course. It was part of the deal. It was why I had pushed for us to get involved with Sean Anderson in the first place. I'm still waiting. *'Sixty Minutes'* got their exclusive party footage for nothing. I had one more reason to be miffed that I wasn't being paid for my part in their show. I console myself with the comfort that the rescuers deserved their drinks and, even if I had planned it otherwise, I'm content to be the guy who ended up paying for them. Nor would I wish to leave a local business out of pocket because of me. Then Sean Fawn-suit arrived to take me back to the hotel. I apologised to Moose for messing him about. The missus was coming to fetch him home anyway. She would be disappointed she didn't get to meet the bloke off the telly. The drive back to the hotel turned out to be the last time I saw Sean. By the following morning he was back with his family. I do not begrudge Sean his familial contentment, but I would have considered it a courtesy for my media advisor to have advised me that he was not going to be around the next day. There were issues which I would have liked to discuss with him.

I still receive wonderful, entertaining e-mails from Moose in New South Wales, often with strange and bizarre videos attached. Lest this be misunderstood, these films include dust storms and giant snakes fighting with mechanical diggers and some bloke dodging death by jumping from one rail track to the other as two trains speed by. We swapped pictures of our children. I envied the guy's domestic happiness as my own circle fell apart. Moose is one of the best.

When I got back to the hotel, I met Tara waiting in the lift lobby. She apologised for not having had a chance to speak to me earlier. It was all about Jamie at the moment. I had no problem with this. Nice lady.

There was a note waiting for me in my room. The crew would come to collect me the following morning after they got back from Jamie's return to the Valley of Near Starvation. I slipped between the sheets of my king-size bed and fell into the untroubled slumber of the mildly enliquored.

Chapter Fourteen

The Homecoming

When I woke up, I was alone. Jamie was out on the trail with the *'Sixty Minutes'* crew. The sun was shining and I got to see the view from my bedroom window for the first time. I looked out on a manicured Australasian paradise. There was a lake, set among trees and bright flowers; parrots flying all around.

Debbie sent a text of congratulation. I started to text back, then thought 'soddit' and gave her a ring instead. This was the Debbie who had taken me and Jeff out for a meal the previous Sunday - the Sunday I had been told that my son was probably dead. Now we shared our amazement at the way things worked out, with my son restored to me, my arse ensconced on a bed as big as an aircraft carrier, newspapers offering crazy money to hear the sound of my voice and parrots flying across the lake outside my window. It had all changed so quickly.

The crew came back to collect me as arranged. We spent the next couple of hours speeding round dirt roads like the Dukes of Hazard, Nick drawling on the phone while turning the wheel with his free hand. They were seeking a suitably spectacular backdrop for final interviews and farewells, determined to shake off all the other news media seeking to compromise their expensive exclusivity. A small convoy of rival newsmen dogged our own small convoy of camera crew, Tara Brown, Jamie Neale and a couple of locally recruited Blue Mountaineers to show the way. It was mildly entertaining - like those *'Wacky Races'* cartoons Jeff and I used to watch in the sixties. Time was running out. I needed to be back in Sydney by about two o'clock to check in for my flight home. We eventually managed to shake off the pursuit and set up camera on a dirt road somewhere near Blackheath. There were some cliffs and a canyon to look at. The road was a dirt track but it still proved to be pretty busy, much to my glee and Nick's frustration. Passing motorists slowed down as they passed by, gawping at their surprise preview of the Jamie Neale documentary.

I breezed through my interview, never at a loss for words, as usual. Backpacker Dad's off-the-cuff bonhomie starkly contrasted with Jamie's more haunted, thoughtful delivery. He came across as much the more mature of the two of us. I produced the hammer and chisel I'd used to carve his obituary on the rocks of Ruined Castle. The bit they must have liked the best was how I described the returnee's eyes as looking like he was about to get run down by a train. At any rate, that was the bit they broadcast.

Then they asked us to walk up the road together like we were engaged in warm, good buddy conversation, finishing up with a fond farewell and a little joke as we gaze out over this unnamed valley which wasn't actually where he got lost. Jamie clearly wasn't entering into the spirit of the business. He was moody and taciturn. After the cameras were off, I handed over various bits that Jeff had brought over from Perth, including Jamie's Duke of Edinburgh wallet. I gave him some more cash and accepted the stuff he wanted me to take home ahead of him. He said how hurt he had been by my threat to cut him out of my will, leave it to the NSPCC. It was odd that he was bringing back words I'd spoken in Muswell Hill, before he'd left Australia, bringing them up at this time and place, beside a dirt road in the Blue Mountains. So much had happened since then. I assured him he would get his inheritance. The ordeal had drawn us closer. We embraced and wished each other 'Good Luck!'

Once again, I had Nick as my chauffeur as we sped away to find the airfield. Nick was mortified to see a rival cameraman quietly waiting by the gate of the airfield ready to get cheap footage of Backpacker Dad boarding the chopper.

The pilot was the same guy who had flown me over the Jamison Valley about a week before. He was a smashing bloke - one of the few media employees whom I felt genuinely comfortable with. At one point, the pilot received an enquiry about a driver coming to pick up Richard Cass.

"Dunno anything about it, mate. Tell him to phone up Channel Nine". Then he turned to me.

"That's some bloke trying to kidnap you," he laughed. "The tricks these guys get up to!"

You get to see an awful lot of bush when you fly over it in a chopper. I had come this way by road, oblivious to the vast acreage of wilderness beyond that ribbon of civilisation. After about twenty minutes of deep, deserted canyons between tree-girt ridges, the scene flattened out and there were houses and cars and schools encroaching on the greenery.

We touched down at Sydney airport and there was yet another camera crew waiting to record my final thoughts before leaving Australia and another blonde to prod them out of me. I was happy enough to go through it all over again. I owed a lot to this country. They drove me to the international departures building and followed me all the way to the point where I went through the security gate. It was embarrassing to stride through the hall to check in like any other passenger, pretending not to notice that there was a TV camera hovering a couple of feet away from my ear.

People recognised me, congratulated me, shook my hand and offered good wishes. A kid about ten years old squealed "It's the man on the telly!" I raised my hat in acknowledgement. Ah, the seductions of celebrity!

At the final portal, where the camera could follow me no further, I was asked for a final farewell speech on the soil of this wonderful country that had brought my son back to me.

"Thank you, Australia!"

I have no doubt it ended up on the cutting room floor somewhere in the bowels of Channel Nine.

I grabbed the usual cheesy gifts to get rid of the last of my Aussie dollars. A cuddly kangaroo for Jean, koala for mum, shots glasses for Clair and a platypus for me. I bought an aborigine rag doll for the school.

I had to pay out A$100 to Thai Airways for rebooking my flight, but the ticket lady said she would make it up to me by getting me a good seat. The seat was in the middle row with an empty seat to the left of me and the aisle on my right. This favour meted out with such honest good intent inevitably rebounded to my discomfort when, in due course, the toddler in front ejected a sinus-rending, eye-watering splodge of diarrhoea. The soiled seat had to be replaced in midair by unlucky stewardesses kitted out in face masks and rubber gloves. No peace for the blessed.

I was later to be accused of abandoning my son in Australia while I rushed home to sell my poisonous tale to the media. At the time I rebooked my flight, I was unaware that Jamie's health would preclude him from flying home for about six weeks. I assumed that he would wish to fly as soon as he got out of hospital and that he would therefore be coming home soon after I made the trip. It was important for me to get home and start earning my living again. I am not a wealthy man. I have a mortgage to pay and numerous other outgoings that would not go away while I dallied in Australia. I also had to earn the money to pay for flights and hotel bills and the notorious bar-tab which had all been stacked up on my credit card. My mobile phone bill was about £400; twenty times what I'm used to! Do my detractors suggest that I should have cancelled my flight a second time, incurring yet another penalty charge, if not a demand that I pay the full cost of my eventual flight home? The suggestion that I rushed home intending to sell my story is untrue. I had no thought of 'going feral' on my son until after I got home. We were clearly getting on one another's nerves. It was probably for the best that I did leave him to it. I was euphorically happy to have him back. He appeared to be suffering some kind of passing melancholia in the aftermath of his ordeal. Unfortunately, nothing grates upon the mind of the miserable than the company of the joyful. I was not leaving him alone in Australia. He was chaperoned by Sean's staff and then he would travel over to Perth to spend time with his uncle and cousins.

We touched down in Bangkok in the middle of the night. I had a couple of hours to kill, so I wandered round the airport shops, browsing rather than looking for anything in particular. In the end, I was tempted by a couple of fridge magnets and a copy of *'The Sun'*.

This casual purchase went on to become one of the fatal links in the chain of causation that led the schism between Jamie and me. *"The Sun"* is a powerful and popular tabloid, part of Rupert Murdoch's 'News Corporation' conglomerate. Politicians tremble at the prospect of falling out with *'The Sun'*. On an inside page, I was astonished to read an acerbic, ill-informed, but brilliantly headlined denunciation of the whole lost backpacker miracle, labeled *'Survival of the Fibbest!'*.

Having spent much of the previous four days in the thick of a jostling, pleading but ultimately on-side media circus, it was quite a shock to read this kind of sceptical twaddle churned out at the expense of my own flesh and blood. I was aware that it was all in the game. The journalists and 'experts' lending their names to this tosh were likely to be well aware that they were peddling piffle. At least *'Sun'* Doctor, Carol Cooper, had the grace to insert the exculpatory qualification *'If I didn't know better...'* as she commented on Jamie's supposed blooming health. *'I'd have thought he'd been out camping for the night'*. Andy McNab, a writer who rose to fame through writing about his own heroics in the First Gulf War, was less guarded. *'I know an SAS lad who died from hypothermia within 36 hours on the Brecon Beacons'*. New South Wales ain't Old South Wales, Andy. It was knockabout stuff, but I was worried that a lot of people would read this nonsense and be convinced there might be something in it. *'The Sun'* is an opinionated and opinion-forming paper with a high circulation. The story was likely to become a kind of tabloid 'Authorised Version' - the definitive account of what really went on in those blue remembered hills, particularly for the impressionable young men and women who would be mixing with Jamie at university. This had to be challenged. I suspected that *'The Sun'* were 'trailing their coat'. In other words they were hoping to provoke a response. They would then get our story and maybe confess that they had got it wrong as a kind of *quid pro quo*.

Years ago *'The Sun'* published a story about Elton John, claiming that he had doctored his guard dogs to stop them keeping him awake with their howling all night. Elton's lawyers got in touch and the *''The Sun'* admitted they had been misinformed and that Elton was a really wonderful bloke. The dog story was followed by weeks of positive copy about *'our mate, Elton'*.

Maybe I could smooch up *''The Sun'*, give them a bit of blustering, 'outraged dad' copy to keep their reporters scribbling. The paper was actually very keen to get in on the inside track of the Jamie Neale story, as I was to find out when I went public with my dispute with the boy. They never came into meaningful contact with me and they will be surprised at the pivotal role they played in the way the story developed. My prediction that what *'The Sun'* writes tends to become the definitive account for many people became all too true at that later time. While I was talking exclusively to the *'Mail on Sunday'*, carefully explaining that I was upset that I had not been paid for work I had done and that I had earmarked the money for the good causes, *''The Sun'* got in first with their sour grapes spoiler, the fictional account of how grasping Backpacker Dad was demanding half his son's money. It was this libelous nonsense which became embedded in the minds of most people. Yet it was a story unsupported by anything I had said, attributed to anonymous 'sources'. The story was picked up and recycled by almost every other news medium. Those same sceptics who prided themselves on not accepting Jamie's survival story at face value had no hesitation in accepting this greedy dad fiction, unsupported by the slightest evidence. It woz indeed *"The Sun'* wot did it!

As I cruised across the Middle East at 30,000ft, I came up with my cunning plan to capitalise on *"The Sun's'* obvious interest in this story. I would offer them my body.

Andy McNab and I could go head to head on an overnight yomp across the Brecon Beacons. Andy would shiver through the night in his long-johns and cable-knit cardigan while I stroll around in shorts and flip flops. I would show McNab of Mesopotamia the stuff my gene pool was made of!

"Fancy another dip in the frigid waterfall, Andy?"

Better still, they could fly us off to Greenland to swim with the polar bears. Cue poor Andy blubbing away on the pack ice in his parka jacket and mittens while I merrily dive back through my hole in the ice, emerging ten minutes later, killer whale pup clenched between unchattering teeth.

"Come on in, Andy. The water's lovely!"

"Okay, Richard. I was so wrong about the cold killing anyone from your family. Can we go home now? Please!"

"Oh okay, Andy. If it's any consolation, old chap, I wouldn't have lasted five minutes in all that Iraqi sunshine!"

'The Sun' is not without a sense of humour.

Of course I also had in mind that I needed to make some money to make up for the way I'd been gypped over the *'Sixty Minutes'* appearance money. People in Australia would see me in the show, hear about how much was paid, then assume I'd got my whack out of it. In due course, investigative reporters would be checking up on whether I had kept my promise to donate the media cash back to Australia. Jamie had placed me in the ticklish situation of having appeared to have made money while not having done so. Even if I explained that the money had all gone to Jamie, this was likely to be dismissed as a collusive device to keep cash in the family. *'The Sun'* could afford to be generous in paying for my story and any prospective pratting around on the Arctic pack ice. I could donate the cash to the hospital or SRS and my credibility would be safe. Richard, you are brilliant!

As soon as the plane touched down at Heathrow and I'd jumped all the hurdles and hoops to get back into Britain, I rang Jamie to run my idea by him. With considerable whinging reluctance, Jamie said 'alright' but he wanted the *'The Sun'* to be absolutely certain that I was not speaking on his behalf. I thought this worry was unnecessary. Jamie was in Oz and looked like he was going to be there for at least another month. I was back in the UK. What could be more natural than that an outraged parent would rush to defend his son's honour against such scurrilous piffle?

I made my way across London by tube. The Jamie Neale story had not had quite the same impact in Britain as it had in Oz. No one recognised me. No pressman bothered me for a comment.

But I couldn't resist pointing out the picture in the *'News of the World'* being read by the fat black bloke sat beside me. "That's my boy!"

"Hey yeah! I recognise you!"

I was pretty tired by this stage. The euphoria of the last four days had just about worn off and left me feeling lonely and low. I emerged at Bounds Green with heavy bags and a long walk back to Jean's place to pick up my car. I came bearing gifts, sure of a warm, triumphant welcome when I got there. I shouldered my bag and crossed over the road.

It was just as I got to the other side when I got the text that changed everything.

"Chatted with Sean. Dont' do the complaint. I can fight my own battles dont need my dad to defend me. can sort it out when I'm in uk. Anything you say we'll have the impression from me anyway. He said they would go feral and just we know the truth. fuck em. Andy mcnab is a war author anyway, aint proper squaddie. 'love' Jamie" (sic).

It was this text that lit the blue touch paper that exploded the firework and sent it cartwheeling out of control. It took a bit of time to work its poison on my soul. My first reaction was stupefaction that Jamie could not see the sense of getting *'The Sun'* on our side. Lest I receive a libel writ, delivered by a man swinging from a rope crashing through my bedroom window, I must first of all state that, unlike my son, I have no reason to doubt that former SAS soldier McNab did indeed covertly parachute into Iraq during the First Gulf War.

As I trudged my weary way through the streets north of Ally Pally, my emotions became darker. I had asked for Jamie's go-ahead, not as a subordinate begging permission but as a courtesy. The rescinding reply came back in the imperative mood. My son was giving me an order. Not *'I'd rather you didn't'* but *'Dont'* (sic). That raised hackles, as did the medium of text rather than a proper discussion, as did the chat with Sean. It had echoes of the private meeting that cut me out of the Channel Nine cash. Sean was my agent as well as Jamie's. If Sean had good reason to dissuade me from contacting the best funded newspaper in the United Kingdom, then it was a shame he lacked the professional courtesy to phone up and discuss it with me, rather than delegate the job to my traumatised teenage son and this piss-taking text message. The stuff about not needing his dad was, to put it mildly, insensitive after I had spent time and treasure in seeking him. I disagreed that Jamie could effectively sort anything out when he got back a month after the offending article had been published. I disagreed that the public would assume I was not talking for myself and I disagreed that my involvement would send *"The Sun'* feral'. *'Survival of the Fibbest'* was clearly about as feral as it could get. I was shocked that a young man on the brink of undergraduate education could make such a horlicks out of spelling a simple word like 'will'.

I was Jamie's father. I was not obliged to ask his permission about anything, but I had done so. I could not now proceed with my plan to contact *'The Sun'*. Next time, I would not bother to seek Jamie's agreement if the reply was likely to be couched in such an offensive tone. Indeed, the notion that anything I said would be assumed to reflect his own point of view would apply to just about any approach I made to the UK media. I was being gagged. I assume that Jamie was unhappy about the way my insistence that I was not going to keep any money I got from the media was being foisted upon the pair of us. I was happy to clarify that these promises were not binding on my son.

The most toxic aspect of this fateful text message was not to be found in the actual words, but the punctuation. The word 'love' was bracketed between a pair of inverted commas. Inverted commas are used for a number of purposes - to denote that a word is slangy or unconventional, to indicate a quotation within a sentence. But the only possible interpretation of this particular pair of commas was that they were intended to express irony; that Jamie's 'love' was not to be taken at face value. I have no real idea why Jamie chose to qualify his chosen form of sign-off in this manner. If he was simply embarrassed to express filial affection, then why not sign off in some other way - 'regards, Jamie' or 'bfn'? Textese is axiomatically brief, with grammar, punctuation and spelling ruthlessly sacrificed to convey the sense of any given message with least jabs of the key pad. Jamie had twice dispensed with the apostrophe in 'don't'. Yet he had then taken the trouble to attach gratuitous punctuation to his love for me.

Dear Reader, you were deceived; lied to over your cornflakes. I did not fall out with my son over anything as trivial as the money. We fell out over a couple of punctuation marks.

Chapter Fifteen

The Betrayal

The following chapter is not an easy one for me to write. I am a proud and opinionated man and it is never easy for me to admit I got it wrong, but I did do wrong in publicising my differences with Jamie. I did so with reluctance. I should have found a way to back down from the threats I made when those threats failed to deliver. I allowed passions to drive my actions in a way that, in the aftermath, I see should have been better controlled. In setting all this down I am not excusing or expiating my behaviour. I am trying to explain it.

One thing needs to be clearly understood. The wrong I did was never done through motives of financial gain. Folk are free to make up their own minds about anything, but no fair-minded person disparages another person's integrity without evidence to back it up. I invite those who accuse me of leeching or money grubbing or exploiting my son to show me the evidence that I ever asked my son for money that I was not entitled to, or evidence that I failed to fulfil my promise to send all the money I got from the media back to New South Wales. I have receipts to prove what I got and where it went. My detractors have nothing to back their opinions but an ignorance of the facts and their general cynicism about human nature. They call me greedy because they see their own Caliban image in their imaginary portrait of me. How many of them would uncomplainingly work for nothing while their partner takes everything? How many of my self-appointed moral censors would cheerfully give away a small fortune in fulfilment of a pledge?

That said, I am ashamed to plead guilty to an assortment of other, perhaps equally shameful, transgressions - blackmail, betrayal, whistle-blowing, mistrust, arrogance, anger and getting things out of proportion. I will never cease to believe I was badly served by my son and former publicity agent, but I should have dealt with things better. I engaged in a game of brinkmanship, without an exit strategy. When neither side was prepared to swerve, we ended up crashing head on with sorry consequences for all concerned. I wish things had worked out differently. I allowed feelings of hurt, dejection and outrage to cloud my judgment.

Having choked back the bitter cud of Jamie's 'dont need my dad' text, I arrived on his mother's doorstep for my triumphal, ticker tape welcome. Eleven days earlier, I had left set out to find a missing son, a missing brother. Now the beloved boy had been found, surely t'was time to hug, rejoice and be thankful?

Or not, as the case may be. There was an odd atmosphere at Jean's place. Not what I had expected. I felt I was an awkward, unwelcome guest for whom politeness must be maintained but whose dalliance should be discouraged. I handed over the cuddly kangaroo. Shots glasses for Clair? She's asleep. You must be tired too. Why don't you just head off home?

Jean clearly knew how things were going. She was taking sides. Was this the end for Jean and me after twenty-two years of intermittent intimacy?

I was as comprehensively out in the cold as if I had indeed gone a-frolicking with those polar bears.

How much did she really know? I was convinced that things were going on behind my back, that I was being 'managed', neutralised, put out to grass. Perhaps, if I had stayed, things might have been different. I wouldn't have been able to e-mail the press about my grievances and things could have been allowed to blow over, but I headed up the M1 to brood alone.

I was woken in the afternoon by a text message from Jamie. It was friendly enough, telling me 'the pretty Irish lass' had been in touch with Sean. This was the lady I'd sat beside on the flight from Heathrow. Such was my mood of outrage that I saw the friendly tone as a belated effort to undo the damage done by the earlier text. Even Jamie now realised that he had made a big big mistake - that my goodwill could no longer be taken for granted.

I sent back an e-mail expressing my disappointment about his veto on approaching *'The Sun'*. From now on, I would not bother to ask his permission but would be touting the story about my breach with him. Let him chew on that!

The reply was a definite attempt at an olive branch. It expressed a kind of gritted teeth apology, an acknowledgement that *"I have been pretty hard on you. I am annoyed at some of the stuff but you did come out and I do appreciate it. I haven't expressed how I feel to anyone other than the immediate family. But hearing you had put the phone down on mum and some of the other stuff has angered me. I am not going to say a bad word about you to anyone. I'm not saying you have done nothing wrong but I am sorry and I hope you accept it. But I'm drawing a line under it. Also Nick did apologise for the thing in the car and said he had been rude"*.

In retrospect I ought to have accepted this pathetic attempt at an apology which seemed to me, in my discontent, to be more a series of vague accusations against me than sincere acceptance of much regretted wrongdoing. Jamie had progressed from contempt to condescension but fallen well short of contrition. The revelation that I was considered to have 'put the phone down on mum' was new to me. It did nothing to appease my anger. What a complete pair of plonkers! When Jean had raised this matter with me, I explained that we had been cut off by a flat battery rather than any curtness on my part. I was surprised she had ever thought otherwise, as I was not aware of any kind of disagreement during my time in Oz that might lead her to think so badly of me. Jamie had never raised the matter with me and I was unaware that Jamie had even been told about it. Jean had not seen fit to tell him it had all been a misunderstanding. Yet now this monumental non-event appears to have been a factor in the animosity I had endured during our last couple of days together! Why hadn't Jamie asked about it in Oz, instead of being *'pretty hard'* on me?

The reference to *'some of the other stuff'* was also hardly calculated to calm me down. How was I supposed to defend myself against that kind of vagueness? At the time, I supposed he meant my shooting my mouth off about handing the money back but I still don't really know. I found Nick's apology a surprise. Did Jamie seriously believe that this was a significant factor in my going Rambo? Why did all the media folk in Australia choose to communicate with me via my teenage son rather than man to man?

Nevertheless I should have gritted my own teeth and accepted that line drawn under the past. I had fired a shot across Jamie's bows and he had attempted, clearly more through self-interest rather than sincerity, to avoid the coming bloodbath. The commitment not to bad mouth me in public or private was a welcome one. I had little to gain by taking things further - except the unfinished business of the deal done behind my back. I went on to insist that some part of that A$100,000 should be paid to me in recognition of my contribution to the documentary. I had provided an interview and staged farewell footage. I had set up the party at Gearin's which had been exclusively filmed by Channel Nine. I had honoured the commitment to exclusivity at a time when there were many other media organisations clamouring for my time. Yet I had got nothing out of all this except a begrudgingly proffered hamburger and a helicopter ride. If my contribution was so insignificant as to be worth zero, why had the chopper been laid on so that filming could continue for that extra couple of hours? I had even been landed with the thousand dollar bar tab which had been my reason for involving the media in the first place!

I wanted to initiate a negotiation. I sent off an e-mail to Sean indicating what I thought of as fair. 'I would have been happy with 15%'. I did add 'not now though'. This was a negotiating gambit - a hint that they should offer something in that region. I would have settled for less. I finally asked Jean to tell Jamie that £5000 would put it to bed. At an exchange rate of 1.40 Aussie dollars to the pound that represents about seven per cent of the original A$100,000. I would even have considered a counter offer, rather than go nuclear. I would not have been happy with a couple of grand or less. I would have turned it down, but I could hardly have gone running off to the papers moaning about how I had been offered so little. It might still be considered not a bad payday for two days work. I did not see this as 'Jamie's money'. I was asking to be paid for my contribution - money that should never have gone to him in the first place. All Jamie needed to do was remit a few thousand to me. The issue would be closed and I would be off the hook with my promises. I felt I was being more than reasonable. Seven per cent is not 'half Jamie's money'. It is not a quarter. Not an eighth. It represents about one fourteenth of the A$100,000 dollars paid out by Channel Nine. I had promised to remit the media money to Australia in the form of donations to either the SRS or the hospital. That was my business. It did not mean I did not deserve to be paid at all. I was also mindful that this conviction that son and agent had pulled a fast one on me was bound to rankle, poisoning my future relationship with Jamie. For the sake of everyone's future happiness he had to redress this grievance.

The clarity of this perspective seemed to me so manifest that I was sure that Sean and Jamie would see that they must put my grievance right through negotiation, rather than risk my going public. Sean would not want to risk the damage to Jamie's marketability. I was wrong. It was a kind of blackmail, though I was asking for a wrong to be put right rather than profit by it. Sometimes the victims of this sort of thing reply as did the Duke of Wellington - "Publish and be damned!" They did. So I did. And I was.

From my own 'sources', long after the rupture, I have some intimation of the thinking behind Jamie's position. He believes that the money was due to him as he was the one whose suffering had attracted media attention in the first place. He was prepared to make selective donations but dad should be content to rejoice at his son's survival. He would pay my expenses. It's not my point of view. I see no real connection between his suffering and his claim to be paid for my interviews as well as his own, but I have no problem with Jamie or anyone else that sees it that way. If Jamie had put it to me that this was the way he wanted it to be and it was important to him, I would have let him have his way. If I'm expected to work for nothing, I just wish to be consulted about whether I consent to it. Instead, it had been imposed as *fait accompli* backed by that humiliating gloat - "because you said you didn't want anything!" Jamie knew perfectly well I was keen to make donations.

It was galling but I had gritted my teeth and played my part in the documentary. I was furious with Jamie, even more furious with Sean for failing to negotiate separate payments, but I lumped it. We were in a hospital. I'd just got Jamie back. It was neither the time nor place for a row.

I knew Jamie was tense and traumatised. Perhaps, when he had recovered, he would regret his churlish behaviour. I was still determined to get something for my story. I felt an obligation to make a donation to those who had given their time to go look for him. I also had visions of reporters turning up on my doorstep accusing me of breaking yet another (!) Pommy pledge to the people of Australia.

Running parallel with this spat with Jamie was my even more rancorous correspondence with Sean. I had gifted Sean my signature at a time when the world's media were laying siege to the pair of us. He held himself out as a professional advisor. I was naturally aware that Jamie was bound to be more 'marketable' than me, but I had promises to keep and plenty of media folk were keen to get a piece of me. This 'professional negotiator' had sold my story for a helicopter ride and a night in a hotel. He then supported

Jamie in his veto of my making contact with the highest paying paper in the United Kingdom, without deigning to speak to me about it. When I asked for explanation, he said that I could not sell my story in the UK, because this breached the deal with Channel Nine. In other words, because my agent had effectively sold my story for zilch in Oz, I could not subsequently sell my story for what it was worth in the UK. I e-mailed Sean to indicate that he was in breach of his contractual duty to 'use best endeavours to maximise all commercial opportunities presented'. He responded by claiming no one was interested in talking to me. *'Remember this story is about Jamie, not you'.*

He went on to say *'Any attempt to take on the newspapers will be futile'*.

In the circumstances, particularly in view of my rapidly escalating ill temper, his choice of the word 'futile' was unwise. It challenged me to refute the assertion. That clicheic boast 'All resistance is futile' retains such a whiff of cod science fiction comedy that it was difficult to take Sean's bluster seriously. I am not too sure what Sean meant by 'futile' in this context. If he sought to convey that it was not in my own interest to contact the media, then I have to admit he was right, though I was not in the mood to take any kind of advice from him by that time. If he meant I would not succeed in getting them to take an interest in me then he was very much mistaken or, more likely, he was bluffing. He knew well enough that they would be ready to bite my hand off in their enthusiasm to hear this story. Bizarrely enough, in the midst of all this ill-feeling, Sean claimed to have negotiated a £1000 interview for me with another 'docco', refuting his own contention that no one had any interest in anything I had to say and thereby also conceding that, as a matter of fact, I was entitled to be paid for this sort of thing. If Sean had deigned to employ similar diligence on my behalf at an earlier stage, things would have worked out differently between us and, even more importantly, between Jamie and me. The offer was probably genuine. Indeed, the relevant company contacted me directly after I ceased to be Sean's client. I was too suspicious to 'take the bait'. Such was my reluctance to trust Sean by this stage, that I suspected he was seeking to trap me into some stunt whereby I appear to accept money, which is he trumps up as media-gotten gains which I failed to pay out as promised. I am sorry it didn't work out for them due to a dispute which was not of their making.

I lit a bit of a firecracker under Sean's arse by e-mailing Channel Nine to say that I was going public about Sean letting me down and I might also be mentioning the unpaid bar bill and Nick's belatedly offered burger. In the end, they broke this scoop themselves to pre-empt me - *'Cass... overlooked for a hamburger order'* (Holly Byrnes, *Sydney Daily Telegraph*, July 25th 2009). They really need not have bothered. It was clearly in their interest, as well as Jamie's, Sean's and mine, to persuade Sean to settle our dispute in an equitable manner. Instead they elected to close ranks with Sean and contribute to the Holly Byrne's picnic-at-hanging-Rick smearfest and these same ratbags still owe me the best part of a thousand dollar bar tab. So much for Nick's passed on apology about 'the thing in the car'

Part of my problem was that I wasn't sure who had the power to concede the money I felt I was owed. So far as I understood it, the money was paid over to Sean, who then creamed off his seventeen and a half per cent and passed the remainder on to Jamie. That being the case, I assumed Sean would be in a position to pass a few thousand dollars on to me as proportionate payment for my contribution. However Sean always insisted that this was something I had to sort out with Jamie. The contract had been with Jamie, therefore only Jamie could pay anything to me. I suspect that it was Jamie who dug in his toes. Stubborn - like his old man. There was to be no concession. No counter offers. No negotiation. It was up to me whether I would follow through with my threat to go public. I still cannot for the life of me understand why Jamie had a problem with undertaking to pay me money to which I was entitled, yet was willing to pay expenses, which I had never asked him for, or the bar tab, which was not his responsibility. If he had handed over a few thousand pounds that I could remit to Australia,

I would then have played my part in the second docco. This alone would have financed that concession to my *amour propre*. Everyone could have been a winner. Instead, we all lost out when they refused to budge and I refused to walk off with my tail between my legs. Those whom the gods would destroy, they first make mad.

In order to put pressure on Sean, I had been in contact with the *'Sunday Mirror'* about my 'falling out' with Jamie. In calmer times I see that the best course for me to have taken at this point was to go through with a *"Sunday Mirror'* interview but, in exchange for getting it for free, they would not touch on the dispute about the *'Sixty Minutes'* money. Unfortunately, this resolution did not occur to me till it was too late. Instead, I contacted a press agency to find out what my story was worth to the *'Mirror'* and quickly found myself at the centre of a bidding war.

I still felt I could not, with honour, talk to *'The Sun'*. I had asked Jamie's permission to talk to them and he had said 'no'. This was to cost me dear in more ways than one. *'The Sun'* was so vexed at not getting the story that they ran a 'spoiler' falsely claiming I was holding out for half Jamie's money - a story which was widely taken up by other news media and got me pulverised on opposite continents. They also offered £8000 for the story, which is three grand more than I got from *'The Mail'*. My honour cost me, or at any rate the Blue Mountain District ANZAC Memorial Hospital, very dear indeed! Had I abandoned all decency and honour, I might have trousered £30,000. That was on offer if I was prepared to express doubts about the truth of my son's story.

A media auction is conducted according to a set of conventions designed to allow each paper to get a sniff of a juicy story, so that they can decide whether it's worth paying for, but only the winner is allowed to publish the 'exclusive'. I agreed to do a deal with the *'Mail on Sunday'* on Tuesday. They came to interview me on Thursday. The story would be published, obviously, on Sunday. Until then, the story was 'embargoed' so far as the other papers were concerned. They knew something was going on but they couldn't publish. However, the disappointed bidders are 'allowed' to publish their own understanding of the story on offer provided they get a genuine quote out of my mouth or the mouth of one of the other principle actors in the story. This is why newspapers habitually hide their 'exclusives' in a hotel. I was back at work and I refused the offer of a hotel. This refusal caused my press agency contact to have kittens. It was stressed to me over and over again that I must say absolutely nothing to anyone who asked me anything. In this regard, the particular ferocity of *'The Sun'* was constantly stressed. They were livid at missing out and were likely to stoop to anything in their determination to run the story. I was therefore given the password - 'jungle'. When *'The Mail'* contacted me they said the password would be 'the flag'. They also told me that the paper's 'dress code' meant I must not wear jeans or black trousers or sport visible tattoos.

In normal circumstances I might find this kind of thing mildly entertaining, but I was thoroughly miserable about the whole business. If I could have withdrawn with honour, I would have done so, but I had made an agreement and I do not break my word.

In the midst of my misery, yet another farcical episode ensued when I couldn't find the receipt for the Gearin's bar tab. I became convinced, by various additional peculiar circumstances that someone had been in my bedroom while I was out at work.

I explained all this to Hannah, at the press agency.

"It's *'The Sun'*! I told you what they were like! You must report it to the police. That way they can't use it".

So it was that Hertfordshire Constabulary found themselves filling out what has to be a pretty unique crime report - concerning the theft of one Australian bar-tab receipt. They even said they would send someone round to investigate. Having lived most of my adult life at the mercy of 'The Met', it was a shock to discover that there are actually police forces who take the investigation of petty crime at all seriously. I rang back later to report that the receipt was safe and well and that it had all been a terrible mistake and I was very sorry for wasting their time.

Hannah was right about the reporters on my doorstep. It is not easy to slam the door in people's faces when they are so beseechingly polite but I did what I had to do. I saw one poor lad rush over from his car in the middle of a downpour. He rang the bell and stood there with heavy rain drenching him to the skin.

"Mr Cass? I'm from *'The Daily Express'*..."

I ran an imaginary zip across my lips and closed the door.

There were about five of them in all. No one from *'The Sun'* though. *'The 'Sun'* lived up to their dastardly reputation, saved themselves the trip up the M1 by gulling an embargo busting quotation out of Jean.

"He's disgusting. How can he do this to his own son?"

The cat was well and truly out the bag but it wasn't the same moggy I'd put in there. The story was not *'High Minded Arsehole of a Father Insists on Token Payment for Docco Appearance'*. It was *'How can this Greedy Scumbag of an Excuse for a Father Demand Half Bush Survivor's Cash?'* "Richard Cass is said to have flipped after the teenager refused to hand over half the cash". *Au contraire, mes amis*. I took Jamie's 'You're getting nowt!' snub on the chin. I actually flipped when I was denied my place in *'The Sun'*. Interestingly, *'The Sun'* still suspected a scam. It was my 'LOST' (sic) son who 'cut me out of £50K deal'. Those inverted commas are the typographic determinative of a raised eyebrow.

Jamie and I were reported to have fallen out after Jamie reneged on an agreement to split the cash in two. We were, in journalese shorthand, 'fighting over the money'. Where did this 'half the money' nonsense come from? To be fair to Sean, he was later quoted as confirming 'a rift' but 'I am not in a position to go into details'. Does the notion of splitting or sharing money necessarily imply a fifty-fifty split? Jeff rang from Oz on Saturday to warn me that things had turned very ugly. I told him I'd had an interview with *'The Mail'* on Thursday and that my version would come out on

Sunday. He was wise enough to say I should not have done it and that my own high-minded perception of the issue would not stand up against the tidal wave of bile foaming my way. People could not cope with that kind of complexity. It was a dispute about money, therefore I must be greedy. To sulk about money when my son had been found alive and hundreds of people had bust their guts to find him was not going to go down well and nothing I said would make a blind bit of difference. It was a shame I hadn't spoken to Jeff earlier in the week.

The actual interview with *'The Mail on Sunday'* had been a bit of an ordeal, though they were, I believe, genuinely sympathetic to the way I had been treated, particularly by Sean. I made no attempt to denigrate my son. I made it clear that I was unhappy about the way I had received no payment for my part in the Channel Nine documentary and that I had not wanted the money for myself. I loved and admired my son and all I ever wanted was for him to do the right thing and we could all be happy again. I understood that he had not been feeling himself after his terrible ordeal. Although I reserved my outrage for Sean Anderson, they made it clear that Sean's conduct was off limits. This was a father and son dispute. That was the 'human interest' angle. They told me what a rare delight it was to speak to a newsworthy member of the public who could not only express himself so well but who also had a well-stacked book case in his living room. The photographer took my photo beneath glowering thunderclouds, standing beneath the wisteria on the patio that Jamie helped to build. I rolled down my sleeve to cover my tattoos. Next day I got a phone call. They needed to check something.

"Can you confirm that you really do live in an ex-council house?"

On Sunday I bought the *'Mail on Sunday'*. Under the catchpenny headline of *'I have been robbed by my own son'*, I read Elizabeth Sanderson's reasonably sympathetic condensation of our two hour interview. I was *'a determined, some might say dogmatic man'*. We were *'locked in a feud about money'*. But then there was positive stuff about what a brilliant son he was and how joyful I was to find him. They had spoken to Sean/Jamie and printed what was to become their standard response - *'I do not plan to get into a slanging match with my father but I will say this. I had an agreement with him regarding his 60 minutes interview - he wanted his flights and the party paid for. I agreed to that and intend to honour that commitment'*.

I have carefully considered whether Jamie could, in some strange way, have misunderstood me in thinking we ever had any kind of agreement as opposed to a non-committal response to his offer. People can kid themselves about such things and Jamie was in low spirits at the time this was all happening. I will not therefore accuse him of falsehood, but I do not break agreements. If we had agreed to this kind of deal or any other, I would have kept my word. I should have unequivocally said 'no' at the time he made the offer. He took my silence for assent. When Holly Byrnes wrote her unimaginably inaccurate and hostile piece for the Aussie *'Telegraph'*, accusing me of rushing back to cash in on Jamie's story ('It is understood'), reneging on my no-profits hypocrisy ('It is believed') and daily bathing in the blood of freshly slaughtered koalas ('Sources say'), she was still sufficiently 'off-message' from the Sean/Jamie line to describe me as being 'not content with Jamie's *offer* of expenses'. Someone was spoiling for a slanging match, whatever Jamie might say. Even the reference to expenses was pure spin. 'He wanted his flights and party paid for. I agreed to pay them'. This gives the misleading impression that I petitioned my son for payment as a *quid pro quo* for missing out on the media money. My version would be 'Cass was worried about his expenses. Jamie offered to pay them'. This question of expenses was not one I wanted to discuss in the media. Not because I had anything to hide, but because I recognised that it was a ploy to insinuate that I was a petty, penny-pinching curmudgeon who begrudged laying out a few thousand quid while his son was missing. When I trudged back to the airport on the day he was found, I did not know that there would be any media money coming my way nor that my then missing son would offer to pay my flight bill. If I was that bothered about the costs of flying out to find my son, why did I rush to do so?

As one of my armchair detractors put it, "I wish Cass would stop going on about his expenses!"

Couldn't agree with you more, mate!

What I was up against was not my son squaring up for a 'slanging match' but a monstrous manufactured simulacrum of myself, screaming distastefully for his half share while whining about expenses and not getting a burger. I was being shadowed by this 'Alien-Richard' who's jumping up and down bawling "Handover half the money!" Alien Richard wants the money for himself, of course. Alien-Richard wants someone to pay his expenses... and all this while poor bloody Earthling-Richard runs around, like Burt in that 70's *Soap*, pleading "Listen to me! Please listen to me. Whatever you do - Don't listen to me!"

Why did people believe these canards?

In the wake of Holly Byrnes's 'Dad Demands 50%' article there were one hundred and thirty readers' online responses. Only one of these bloggers had the wit to wonder whether they were reading the whole truth of the matter. I had been sucked against my will into that enduring national epic: *'Ungrateful Pom takes Aussie blood, sweat and treasure for granted'*. God help me if I'd chanced to sport a well-manicured moustache and spoke like Fanny Craddock. Disappointingly, no one brought up Hamilton of Gallipoli, Percival of Malaya or even Jardine of Bodyline. I was assigned to some lesser circle of ungrateful Pommy bastards, shackled to a bloke who survived in an upside down boat off the south coast of Tasmania. God knows what Tony Bullimore did or didn't do to be sneered at in the same blog's-breath as me. It was all such utter nonsense. I had fallen out with my son precisely because I was so determined not to break my pledge to the Blue Mountain community. I had proof of that unvarying commitment to donate my media earnings in the acerbic e-mails I exchanged with Sean and Jamie before I went public.

It was not easy for journalists to get hold of me; easier by far to hear both sides of the dispute as packaged by media agent Sean. Richard or, as

I would have it, Alien-Richard demands half his son's cash while Jamie piously insists he will settle up privately. Readers were no doubt misled into assuming that the real Richard was behind Alien Richard's demands, that journalists were getting both sides of the story from both sides of the story. It was like judging a marriage break-up when you only talk to one partner.

On the following Monday, I got another call from Hannah at the press agency. Was I prepared to be interviewed on Radio 5 Live? There was no fee. Okay. I was concerned about the misinformation that was causing such rancour against Jamie and me, mostly against me. I would use the interview as a chance to make it clear that there had definitely been no agreement. I had been presented with a *fait accompli*, though I was happy to state that Jamie did later offer to pay my flight expenses etc. I was also concerned that too many people thought I had wanted the *'Sixty Minutes'* money for myself. I had already been in touch with Andrea at the Blue Mountain Hospital about how I should donate the £5000 I was expecting to receive from *'The Mail'*. She said that the money could be used to upgrade the staff facilities and accommodation. I was very happy with that. I would not normally wish to advertise my donations to anything like this, but the alternative was that I would be accused of pocketing the cash I'd promised to remit to Australia. I had never heard of Victoria Derbyshire as I never listen to Radio 5 Live. They assured me she was ever so famous.

So it was that I ended up explaining myself to Victoria in a dark studio with a big oval table and microphones radiating out to every place setting. They were worried I was going to lay into Sean Anderson live on air and considered making a recording. In the end it did go out live and I managed to state most of what I needed to say. They had also asked if I was prepared to take calls from members of the public. I said no. I did not wish to talk to the kind of nutters who ring up radio stations. I was told that Radio 5 Live listeners are definitely not nutters. In the event, they pulled the crafty stunt of taking calls from the public but it was Victoria who actually spoke to these people and invited my response. This provided the one telling moment in my brief but blazing media career when I was stumped for words. Craig from Merseyside, or whoever it was, remarked how sad it was that such a wonderful story had ended up in an argument about money. I replied that it was not about money. "I'm not interested in the money. It's about..." Well what was it all about?

"The principle?" suggested Victoria.

No it wasn't about the principle either. It was about finding yourself with heavy bags and a long walk ahead and the brilliant boy you love so much sends a text that says he don't need you no more, old man, then sticks inverted commas round his love for you. How could bloody platitudinous, judgmental Craig from Merseyside ever understand what this was all about?

And, for the time being, that was my final involvement with the media. Reporters turned up on my doorstep from time to time or sent me e-mails and, of course, I got more enquiries from Hannah at the press agency - even Radio One wanted me to speak to me! But it was time to let things calm down. I refused them all. Unfortunately, when you refuse to speak to the media, they get their own back by writing crap about you, either through malice or misunderstanding. I was particularly upset when the story was covered by the *'Muswell Hill Journal'*. This would be read by many of the colleagues I knew at the Special Needs School. It was the usual 'balance'. Richard thinks he should have half the money, Jamie offers expenses. This school, along with the adjoining mainstream school, had held a collection for me while I was out searching. I had to assure everyone that the story was nonsense. I can only pray that they believed me. I was also sick to the heart to think that the rescuers whose hands I had shaken on trails through the Blue Mountains might also be reading and probably believing similar fiction.

It took six weeks to get paid by *'The Mail'* and I immediately sent the money to the Blue Mountain District ANZAC Memorial Hospital. I was just in time. They e-mailed back to say reporters had been in touch to check whether I had donated anything. They were presumably checking up on Jamie's donations too.

Press and blog explanations of my actions were generally ascribed to some deep seated moral failing which afflicts me, some fatal flaw which sets me apart from my fellows. For Elizabeth in *'The Mail'*, I was 'dogmatic'. Other judged me as obsessively greedy, jealous, dysfunctional, ungrateful and monumentally blind to my good fortune in getting my son back.

The last canard was particularly absurd. Of course I was glad he didn't die. Are these idiots assuming that, when I turned metaphorical cartwheels outside that hospital in Katoomba, I was secretly wishing he was still out there? To put it even more crassly, given the choice between (a) a son who is dead and (b) a son who expects me to co-star in his documentary for free, I would be very, very likely to choose 'b'.

As Elizabeth put it *"After such drama, you might expect relief and gratitude, yet these are not the emotions inspiring Mr Cass now"*. Actually, I am full of relief and gratitude, but there is an important point to be made about the gap between what *'you might expect'* and what actually happens in situations of extreme emotional stress.

What I am suggesting is that the way I behaved was not particularly different from the way many other people would behave in similar emotional circumstances. As Elizabeth states, there is a supposition that when a long lost son comes back from the dead, the only possible reaction is unalloyed gratitude, joyous relief on both sides that things did not end in tragedy. Reality is more complex. I was in a state of bliss throughout the time I was with Jamie in New South Wales. Jamie was, on his own admission, down in the dumps. He was very far from the cheerful and confident young man who had set out on his travels about three weeks earlier. He was at times, moody, tearful, brooding and touchy. I believe this is not an unusual reaction to the kind of experience he had endured. He made a good physical recovery during the three days he was in hospital, but he was certainly not as overjoyed to see me as I had expected. In this post traumatic mood, my own happiness became an affliction to him. He was obsessively troubled by my commitment to pay money back to Australia. My insistence that we needed to sign an agent in order to have somewhere to go and to pay for the party rankled with him. He felt 'bounced'. I am sorry about that. I thought it was for the best. He also nurtured a grievance about my supposedly cutting off his mother on the phone. I was, of course, aware of Jamie's low spirits and while I was in Australia, I made allowances for his condition. I understood that he had been through a dreadful and prolonged period of fear, isolation and want and that it would take time for him to recover physically and mentally from the ordeal. When he disappointed me by cutting a deal behind my back, I let it go. When he went out of his way to disparage me on camera, I made little fuss.

However, it must be conceded that I also was not in a 'normal' state of mind. I was fired up with adrenalin. When I was in the squad car, between Sydney airport and the police helicopter pad, I took a call from Gary back in London. He spoke about the money Jamie might make. At the time I was in a state of high excitement, having heard of Jamie's survival only a half hour earlier. Within a flash, I was screaming abuse down the phone. Believe me, gentle reader, that is not how I normally behave.

Jamie's last fatal assault on my complaisant mood occurred when I read the text outside Bounds Green Station. It hit me when I was at my lowest ebb, having not slept for twenty four hours of long distance air travel. I was tired, loaded with a heavy bag and had a long walk ahead of me. I was experiencing a kind of emotional 'come down' after four days of euphoria. My last chance to make some money was brutally and insultingly snatched away. I had public promises to keep and nothing with which to keep them with.

I reacted like a cast off lover. I loved Jamie as a son, of course, but I loved him and cherished him as much as any father who has watched a son blossom from a baby to a man, a man similar, in so many ways, to himself. This time I was, literally, in no mood to let it go.

From time to time, we all hear of episodes of bizarre and extreme acts of madness committed by otherwise rational individuals who find themselves in the kind of emotional vortex I entered that day. The consequences may be mildly amusing for the uninvolved - expensive suits slashed to ribbons, possessions thrown out in the street. Or they may be deeply tragic - victims maimed by knives or acid, wives strangled. In 1963, the promising playwright, Joe Orton, was hammered to death by the lover whom he wished to gently disengage from. A witty put down in Orton's diary was enough to precipitate that tragedy. I was never close to violence in my own anguish and I am certainly not excusing or condoning acts of violence or vandalism. I am simply stating that relationships generate powerful emotional responses when things don't work out as one side or other may wish. It is easy for the calm bystander to say 'I wouldn't do that if I were you'. If I had been well rested and free of the effects of adrenaline, I too might do things differently. The person undergoing the emotional pain cannot step back and behave calmly when their blood is awash with adrenaline and there is a great big knot of anguish squirming inside them. Every smile becomes a sneer. Every inattention, a deliberate and dastardly slight. Every attempt to help, a patronising and unwelcome intrusion. Disputes and discourtesies bite like acid into the psyche.

I recognise that I did things last July that, in the calm of this beautiful autumnal October afternoon, I now recognise as crazy.

What I did was not what normal people do in normal circumstances, but it is not that unusual for normal people to react in extreme and obsessive ways when they are in the throes of rejection from someone whom they love. I am not seeking anyone's sympathy or forgiveness. However, I would appreciate it if people ceased to blame my conduct on a lust for money. For truth is important and that happens to be about as far from the truth as it is possible to get. The truth was almost the opposite of the media storm scenario. I had become, if anything, pathologically obsessed with a mission to fulfil my promise and channel money back to Australia, blinded to the ancillary damage I was inflicting on myself and my family.

Chapter Sixteen

The Rebuttal

One of the sundry delights to offset the downs that followed from Jamie's big fat Aussie adventure was amazement that this son of mine could conjure his very own copper-bottomed conspiracy theory out of a witless bushwalk. That my delightful but dingbat boy should end up there with Di, Marilyn, JFK and footprints on the moon (yeah, yeah...) must be worth a belly laugh or two to soothe my howling anguish. Nobody died. No one got shot, or thrown to the dingoes. There were times it may have felt that way.

During those crazy days when I was hawking this tale of father and child disunion around the British news media, it was put to me that the money on offer might be spectacularly uplifted if I was prepared to express any lingering doubt that my son's story was genuine. I have never had the slightest doubt on that score and I was certainly not going to put on the pretense of such misgivings for all the money in Fleet Street.

There are people who believe that Prince Philip arranged for Diana's car to collide with a particular pillar on the Pont de l'Alma Tunnel. There are others who reckon the Dagenham Girl Pipers plotted 9/11. Nothing I say will make a difference to those who can flag up a conspiracy out of any given cock-up. In their eyes, I am part of the conspiracy and, as such, every syllable I speak or write is compromised. If I cannot bring myself to admit that we faked it, even after I became dangerously disenchanted with the dear boy, then maybe the break-up itself must be part of the master plan, to keep the media in a froth, to make even more money; that maybe the two of us get together every now and then to chortle over our treasure then drink to the liberality of those whom we have gulled. In the fantasies of these diehards I may feature as some kind of reluctant messiah. One day Cass will confess that the two of us dreamed it all up over a pint in the Six Bells in East Finchley, waiting for the quiz to begin. Or maybe someday somebody stumbles upon that cave of Coke tins and Mars bars floating out there in their imaginings, biding time, like Lasseter's gold, at the back of beyond.

There are features of this story which, in the absence of other, more compelling, evidence might give grounds for doubt. The hero is an ostensibly intelligent young man about to embark on three years at Exeter University. Like most students with cash strapped parents, he was worried about the prospective costs of higher education in a year when the economic climate had lurched from unprecedented prosperity to recession. Born in 1989, he was too young to remember the last time that jobs were hard to find. For him, economic depression was something studied in history class - Jarrow Marchers, Hoovervilles and Adolf Hitler. Jamie's prospects of getting a job while studying and then getting well-paid work after graduation had both been adversely affected by this deterioration in the British economy. Why not engineer some kind of newsworthy stunt and let the international press pack foot the bill for the next three years of philosophic engagement?

That oh-so-poignant picture of Jamie posed wistfully beside the world's fattest koala becomes, for conspiracy theorists, a brilliant exercise in media manipulation.

Here's the story as heart-rendingly reported by the Australian *'Daily Telegraph',* generally a likeable tabloid which bears very little resemblance to its British namesake.

> "*Posing beside a koala at a Sydney wildlife park, this could be the last picture the family of Jamie Neale see of their lost son.*
>
> *The 19-year-old British backpacker, on his first overseas adventure alone, e-mailed the image to his sister just in case his camera was stolen. Now it has become a precious keepsake after Jamie went missing during a trip to the Blue Mountains.*
>
> *(Report by Charles Miranda, July 10th 2009).*

It was articles like this, with accompanying image of the missing, dew-eyed waif that brought such a response in terms of record number of volunteers who participated in the search. I am forever indebted to those wonderful men and women and grateful to papers like '*The Telegraph*' for the publicity which kept the plight of my son so much in the public eye. It must be pointed out, however, that almost every assertion in this report was inaccurate. The pictures e-mailed to sister Clair were amateurish snaps which Jamie had taken at the wildlife park; a kangaroo, an emu and a bird of prey. They were all looking either bored or irritated. The e-mail had been sent without accompanying text or even a 'subject'. The koala picture had been taken by a professional photographer, paid for by Jamie, and retained in the form of a mounted print. The police had found this picture, together with Jamie's other belongings at the YHA in Katoomba. The picture was recent and of excellent quality, so it was released to the press by the police for identification and publicity purposes. It was the same picture which had been e-mailed to me to confirm that the missing boy was my son. My point is that neither Jamie nor myself had anything to do with the emotive and slightly misleading way this picture was presented in '*The Telegraph*' and, if we'd planned it, Jamie would certainly have left some sort of appealing message in that last e-mail to the sister he adores. And, ironically, he would not have lost the camera he took with him on his extended bushwalk.

Jamie arrives in Oz and cuddles up to the marsupial icon. He could be anyone's kid, enjoying a first independent holiday, doing the kind of cheesy things we all do abroad. Then comes that bolt from the blue. Maybe dead, maybe still hanging on there. But the longer this goes on…

This story played out into what hard-boiled newsmen call 'a boy down a well'. This denotes a news story with strong emotive content that goes on for a week or so - tearful mum, desperate dad, rescuers by the bus-load, but ... will he make it? Or won't he? These stories sell papers.

This 'boy-down-the-well' topos is sufficiently familiar to have formed the basis of an episode of *'The Simpsons'*. Ironically enough, it begins with a hoax boy-down-the-well scenario set up by Bart who drops a microphone down a well and calls for help. While rescue parties labour to retrieve the supposedly trapped 'Timmy O'Toole', celebrities as diverse as Krusty the Clown and Sting queue up to caterwaul tributes to the trapped kid, 'sending their love down the well'. Bart himself later becomes genuinely trapped down the well when an attempt to conceal his responsibility for the hoax goes wrong. I hesitate to record it but, yes, my son is a *Simpsons* fan.

Jean's failure to break down and cry in front of the cameras was cited by some bloggers as evidence that she knew her son was okay all along, despite the consensus that he was dead. In a sense they were right. The fact is Jean always had faith that her brilliant son had the resources to survive whatever the bush threw at him. I had seen the cliffs and I had seen the search. I was frustrated that I could not get her to understand that he must be dead. I had lost hope. She argued with me. She worried that my pessimism would compromise police willingness to keep on searching. Jean never accepted that Jamie was lost to her.

Some people found my own intervention and antics suspicious. I was articulate, entertaining and I spoke in well-crafted sound bites whilst retaining the air of a media ingénue:-

"The cold won't kill 'im. That boy could run to the South Pole in his underpants,... I'm as English as an Oxo cube".

These comments were of course delivered when I was supposed to be in depths of worry and despair. When I spoke these things I still had hope. I welcomed the publicity as the means of encouraging searchers to keep volunteering and to pressurise the police to keep looking. Some may have seen me as strangely flippant under the stress of prospective bereavement. People cope with extreme situations in different ways. Eventually, those passing days of massive effort by the search teams with nothing to show for it all left even my ebullience ragged. Jean never gave up.

After Jamie had returned, my comments on the boy's mind-boggling folly in failing to take along his phone, or decent map, or adequate food or even that especially purchased space blanket were also 'good copy'. The line about wanting to throttle the lad "but that would spoil the point of him coming back" was also well-received. It was as though I expressed the exasperation of every parent in the face of filial imbecility, alloyed with relief that the prodigal boy had somehow muddled his way back home.

I was quick to learn how the media did its business. Just before I flew back to the UK, I was met by a Channel Nine camera crew waiting to interview me as I stepped from the helicopter at Sydney Airport. As we went through the motions, I heard the sound of a plane in the distance and paused in mid-sentence. "Hey", said the lady holding the mike. "You know how we work!"

She was clearly surprised that such a freshly minted celebrity as myself could pick up the conventions of news camera work so quickly. I did find it fascinating to watch the media folk go about their business. I like to watch the news when I get the opportunity. It was interesting to be in a position to watch the process of assembling a few minutes reportage from the camera crew's point of view. It was a revelation to see how much was recorded and then simmered down to create a few seconds of broadcast news. The biggest surprise was watching interviews. The interviewer runs through her script of questions twice - the first time to record the interviewee's responses, the second time to record the face of the interviewer putting the same questions. Of course the interviewee only answers the questions on the first recording. The two recordings are then interwoven to create a plausible two-way conversation. The technique means only one camera is needed to flip between questioner and respondent. It also leaves me pondering whether the technique is open to abuse. You could be vigourously agreeing to one proposal, then the question gets changed in the run-through and you appear to agree to something else.

There were plenty of sceptics who found it fishy that the 'lost' British backpacker should just happen to have a media-savvy "Backpacker Dad". It seemed just too good to be true from the news media point of view. They were more used to the inarticulate, the platitudinous, the emotional or the aggressive when vox-popping the Great British public. I was soon to overreach myself in my understanding of the intricacies of handling the media.

'Is Richard Cass the world's Coolest Dad?' asked Stuart Jeffries in *'The Guardian'*.

Well, no. And emphatically not so after he went feral on the dear boy. It is a good idea to consult the kids before praising the parent. From the cultivated stereotype of delighted dad, exasperated by my son's antics but eternally grateful to get him back again, I was recast as 'dysfunctional dad', grasping, greedy, ungrateful dad; a dad so demonically obsessed by Channel Nine's unproffered gold, as to be oblivious to the precious gift of a son vouchsafed unto him by God. The press who had lauded my former incarnation rushed to offer their two penn'orth on Backpacker Dad's freshly exposed villainy. It was though I had drunk a potion to emerge from behind the desk with wild eyes and hairy hands. One correspondent compared me to the Jewish grandmother who supposedly berated God after her drowning boy washed back to the beach in answer to her prayers. "He had a hat!" I didn't want Jamie's hat back or even his money. I wanted him back with his conscience intact. I had my own hat.

The press was bad and misinformed enough. The comment that followed the news was about as vituperative and gullible as it gets. The nonsense about me 'walking out' on Jamie when he was three years old was cited from the angle that he'd been lucky to be shot of me. My avarice was stressed, often in contrast to Jamie's assumed youthful virtue.

Mike of Melbourne was typically witless "The kid did donate money to the emergency services... it is his dad who is obviously the money hungry leech trying to cash in on his son." Then there was Bob of Tasmania, "People reading this story have glossed over that he (i.e. Jamie) donated the proceeds of the sixtyminutes program and shouted them a drink as well. It was his father that was upset that he didn't get a cut. Lets show the Poms how ignorant we are but not reading the full story!" (Sic).

Dear Bob, from the perspective of this particular Pom, still clutching his receipt for A$1000 worth of drinks downed at Gearin's and committed, unlike my son, to donating every buck I get to the hospital or the SRS - though of course I didn't get any for my appearance in that *sixtyminutes* show - your ignorance of what you're balls-aching on about is probably about as profound as it gets. It was a case of garbage-in-garbage-out or, to wax philosophical, erroneous conclusions drawn from false premises. Cass wants half the money. Cass wants it for himself. Cass is getting paid for expenses. Ergo, Cass is a greedy scoundrel.

I can't leave this entertaining subject without cocking my snook at bloggess 'Aussie Sheilah of Mona Vale':

"I remember him telling us he was only interested in getting his son back ha ha".

Dear Aussie Sheilah, then you obviously failed to notice other emotions which I expressed at that time, such as the grateful impulse to hand all my media cash to the folk who searched for Jamie - which I did. So ha ha back to you, yer cackling harridan!

More or less contemporary with the unfolding tale of my rift with Jamie, was the much darker and more deeply tragic report of the violent death of 'Baby P'. This child suffered months of torment through the attentions of his mother's sadistic partner, before dying from a spinal injury at the age of seventeen months. Ironically, this despicable crime took place only a mile or two away from my son's home in the London Borough of Haringey. Like Baby P's killer, I had moved in with a divorcee and her children. Unlike him, I did not torture or torment anyone. Nevertheless, anyone perusing on-line comments about the problems between my son and I would have been hard put to say which of these 'dads' was the greater scoundrel. I have to admit I got a kind of ghoulish buzz out of reading their ill-informed drivel.

The problem was that it is not that easy to stereotype a man who insists on being fairly paid for what he performs, despite further insistence that he only wants the money so he can give it away. It was all too sanctimonious, too incredible, too weird for *Australopithecus Bloggensis* take seriously. They needed heroes and villains, not high-minded idiots arguing about who should donate money to whom. When I was interviewed by Victoria Derbyshire on Radio 5 live, I told her that I had studied philosophy at Leeds University in the eighties and that Jamie intended to study philosophy, with economics, at Exeter. It was an attempt to explain how the two of us could follow uncompromising courses of action which were to prove so destructive to both of us. As a philosophy graduate, I understood why Socrates was content to swallow hemlock rather than refrain from telling young Athenians that they knew bugger-all about anything and that the best that they could aspire to was to accept their own ignorance. Philosophers are not the kind of people the general public warm to.

Even Jamie fell afoul of the way the best of intentions can come cartwheeling back like boomerangs to sock you in the eye. He was widely reported as having promised to donate half his '$200,000 cut' from Channel Nine to the rescue service. He did donate something but, of course, nothing like A$100,000. There were even on-line polls asking "Should Jamie keep his promise to donate $100K to the SRS?"

Well, if he promised to do it, of course he should. The fact is he had made no such promise. We had asked Sean to be sensitive to our desire to pay back something to the SRS and this was why the reported '$200,000 deal' with Channel Nine included $100,000 of 'free' advertising for the SRS. Jamie had told a few people at the Gearin's bash how pleased he was that the SRS were getting half the money from the deal. Through misunderstanding this complex commercial arrangement, the pseudo-promise was born. We would have been better off keeping our mouths shut and just handed the money over when we got it. People might then have been pleasantly surprised to get anything at all, rather than fulminate over misunderstood intentions. A number of outraged taxpayers insisted we should be *'made to handover'* everything we took from the sale of our stories. I did not need to be 'made' to do anything. I was doing it willingly and I had never wavered from my stated intention to do just that. Apart from an orange and a ham sandwich, I personally had not cost the taxpayer anything. Okay, maybe a helicopter ride. I had not got myself lost. The failing for which I ought to be made to pay was, presumably, the impregnation of Jamie's mother back in 1989. For my own part, I had paid good, hard-earned pounds sterling for my air tickets, hotel and car hire and international call charges, motor way fines. I had bought two lots of beer for the searchers. Most of this significant expenditure fetched up in Aussie taxpayers' pockets. Footage of me hovering over the Jamison Valley and capering on that hospital patio had been sold around the world, making hundreds of thousands of dollars for Aussie News organisations – money that lubricated the Australian economy, money that paid taxes to the Aussie government. I do not begrudge them their bonanza. I handed over my £5000 of Mail on Sunday cash to the Blue Mountain Hospital. I had nothing more to give. I had not gypped the people of Australia. My Aussie agent had sold the international rights to my story to Channel Nine, while I got paid less than nothing. This same Aussie company had offered to pay for the drinks party, then left me holding the A$1000 bill. Who gypped whom? It has to be said that neither the Rescue Service nor the hospital solicited donations from either of us, or complained about not getting anything or too little. It was newspapermen and Joe Public who belly-ached.

Even more farcical was the trouble caused by my statement in the *'Mail on Sunday'* that 'I can pay my mortgage'. This was meant to convey that I was not desperate for money. Therefore, unlike my son, I could afford to forego my media money in favour of the deserving causes. I was earning enough through regular work to pay my monthly outgoings. For Jamie, the case was different. He was about to struggle with rent, tuition fees and other expenses. The motivation to keep something back for himself was perfectly understandable. Incredibly, some persons - known personally to me - interpreted the quote as meaning 'because I've earned all this media money, I can now pay off my mortgage'. I wonder, aghast with horror, what proportion of the general public were similarly flummoxed!

The sad thing about this interplay between truth, media and public perception was that there were clearly plenty of people ready to take Jamie's tale of survival with a healthy pinch of salt. I have no problem with this. They happen to be wrong but they are right not to take it all on trust. I hope that what I have written here is enough to refute the idea that this was a 'set-up' in the judgment of any fair minded person. But I am also entitled to ask what happened to all that healthy scepticism when it came to the real media con - the tale of Richard Cass, grasping greedy backpacker dad, demanding half Jamie's cash? No one had ever heard or recorded me saying any such thing. It was complete media fiction. I happened to be in dispute with my ex-publicity agent at the time. That alone ought to have flagged up a pause for thought. I suspect that if an opinion poll were conducted on the question "How much of Jamie's money did Richard Cass demand? Was it (a) half (b) none?", probably well over ninety percent would tick the wrong box. The correct answer is 'b', by the way! Why were people so credulous about this canard whilst bone-headedly congratulating themselves on smelling a rat that had been missed by the police, the medics and most of the media? One unfortunate aspect of the 'grasping dad' firestorm was that I opted to turn down the many offers of interview that came to me after the radio appearance. I even got propositions passed to me through Sean Anderson. These knuckleheads carping on about what a scumbag I must be - leave him out in the jungle/desert, don't let this slimy bastard ever darken our sunny shores again - made it too much trouble to do more interviews, collect more cheques to pass on to the hospital and SRS. Yet these credulous fools were often the selfsame people insisting we should pay back every penny spent on the search operation. Their ill-informed fulminations actually made it too much aggro to do just that. Why should I go through two hours or so of private and probing questions, collect the cash to repay our debt to Australia, only to be told it all demonstrated what a greedy old git I must be? And lapping up the limelight too, yer bastard! Dignified silence cost me nothing. It cost thousands of dollars in lost donations to the SRS.

The appreciation that I was not quite the exploitive, Svengalic scoundrel those early spoilers had presented did eventually seep out of the confusion of claim and counterclaim. Even Sydney's *'Daily Telegraph'*, which had published the most inaccurate and vitriolic of the *'Dad Demands Half Jamie's Cash!'* nonsense, seemed to catch on that their 'sources' might not have been telling the whole truth. The focus of Aussie journalistic outrage shifted perceptibly from father to son. Jamie was no longer the gilded youth. He was accused of not having been generous enough with his donations and with not having kept a promise to donate half his Channel Nine cash - the same half share that he had piously withheld from my own grasping avarice. Neither accusation holds water Jamie had not promised anything to anyone. He made appropriate donations which might, in less heated times, have been accepted as reasonable. The Channel Nine promise, like my own demand for half the cash, was a media fiction. Jamie gypped me out of the wherewithal to keep my promise. Neither he nor I gypped the people of Australia.

I suspect that the Sydney *'Telegraph'* were unhappy at the way they may have been misled by Sean's one-sided account of our ding-dong. I am convinced that I had enough to sue for libel and I think they realised it too. Those hundred and thirty odd bloggers baying for my Pommy blood would be a libel lawyer's dream in seeking to establish that his client had been 'exposed to ridicule, hatred, scorn or contempt' and I had e-mails to refute their claim that I had sought half Jamie's cash or that I had reneged on my commitment not to profit.

As if to make amends, *'Daily Telegraph's'* Dave Murray waited outside my house in mid-October and buttonholed me as I stepped from my car. I refused the proffered opportunity to 'put my side', but Murray provoked sufficient self-justificatory comment out of me to cobble together a positive report on the subject of my incredible lack of avarice, which must have come as a surprise to many readers. As I refused to let Dave in the house, I can't complain about the inaccurate reference to a broken agreement. I do whinge about his dig at my ten year old Skoda and modest domicile.

I got a call from Jean at three o'clock the following morning to say that Jamie was unhappy that I had broken cover with these kerbside musings. I also got offers of interview on Aussie TV. They said they got my e-mail address from Sean. I turned them down.

Whilst not wishing to belittle my son's eleven nights of cold, hunger and isolation, references to 'freezing conditions' were just media hype. Night-time temperatures in the Blue Mountain district were never below zero degrees centigrade on any of the relevant nights. Some were near freezing and some were both cold and wet. Jamie certainly suffered from the cold, despite being constitutionally better able to cope than most - something I was keen to tell anyone who would listen, lest they conclude he was dead when he wasn't. One of the health problems he suffered as a result of his ordeal was loss of sensation in his right hand thumb and index finger. He still has difficulty in tying his shoelaces. He was dressed in a t-shirt and buttoned shirt. He set out dressed in a lightweight shower-proof jacket, along with jogging bottoms and trainers. This is certainly not ideal clobber for cold winter nights but was marginally better than the 'flimsy clothing' which some commentators foisted on his back.

There is actually plenty of insulation lying around in the bush in the form of leaf litter, dried fern leaves and stringy bark. There is even some shelter from the rain in the form of rock overhangs and fallen tree trunks.

He was not lost 'up a mountain' but down in the Cedar Creek Valley. In most mountain districts, such as the Alps or Cairngorms, hikers leave their hotel down in the valley and stride out to climb an adjacent mountain peak. In the Blue Mountains it is actually the 'mountain top' which is heavily populated. It is usually necessary to descend to the valley floor to enjoy a decent bushwalk. The towns of Katoomba, Leura and Wentworth Falls are located on the main plateau, so they are more or less at the same altitude as the isolated plateau of Mount Solitary. Descent to the valley involves going down about 300 metres of almost sheer sandstone cliff. You either scramble down one of the few available cliff paths or ride the cliff railway from *Scenic World*. In other words, ambient temperature near the valley floor is likely to be slightly warmer than that experienced in Katoomba town on those cliffs high above. The valley is also more sheltered from the wind, both by the trees and topography. The temperatures endured by Jamie Neale were certainly nowhere near as cold as those experienced by another 'lost child' in the winter of 1866. Two year old Alfred Boulter went missing on a Monday and was found the following Wednesday. On the intervening Tuesday, the Hobart *'Mercury'* reported *'unprecedented cold weather and hoar frost'*. The same periodical also mentioned young Boulter: *'He had wandered away into the bush and has undoubtedly perished'*. After the babe had been found, frostbitten but very much alive, the *'Illustrated Melbourne Post'* asserted that *'the weather was intensely cold, and the nights were more severe than had ever previously been known in Tasmania. The salmon ponds were frozen over enough to bear the weight of a man'*. This lucky waif was inevitably described as having been *'scantily clad'*.

How close was Jamie to reaching the end of his physical endurance when he stumbled into the arms of his rescuers on the morning of the 15th of July? I estimate that he could have survived one more night, possibly two or three. Within that time frame it should have been possible for him to have reached houses and roads on the outskirts of Megalong simply by following the path alongside the power line. The question is whether he had sufficient reserves of motivation to keep going and the sheer physical endurance required of a body that had been deprived of calories for so long. He was lucky enough to meet the campers and not have to do so. I think he would have made it. It is certainly true that the medical advice was inclined to assume that his chances of being alive after twelve days without food were very slim. Some people were surprised that he managed to climb up the cliffs and out of the valley to meet up with the police on Narrow Neck Plateau. It was Jamie's apparent good health that was cited against him by those who refused to be convinced. They were expecting him to be snatched from the valley floor as a gibbering, skeletal wreck. Perhaps he should have carried on walking, just to please the scoffers. After all, Clara Crosbie, at just eleven years old, survived twenty-three days lost in the bush near Melbourne. She was found by chance, lacerated, emaciated and stark naked, just five miles from where she went missing on May the 12th, 1885. Within the year, she was reprising her tribulations at the waxworks opposite Sydney Cathedral. Admission - one shilling. Sixpence for children.

The fact was that though Jamie had been severely undernourished, he had managed to eat 'bush tucker' during his time in isolation. He brought back some pods of the tongue orchid and had also eaten a leafy vegetable 'something like rocket'. He had no idea whether these items were safe to eat, but had little choice but to give them a go. He was incredibly fortunate in that one of the couple that found him was an Australian Army medic, with both knowledge and resources to cope with his severely emaciated condition. It was Jamie's choice to climb out of the valley, rather than wait to be airlifted. Revived by the nutrients he had received, buoyed up by realisation that he had survived the ordeal, he felt he had the strength to tackle the climb up to Narrow Neck Plateau. If it was all a scam, surely he would have hammed up the weakness and got choppered out. Psychologically, he had had his fill of Cedar Creek and wanted nothing more than to be out of it as soon as someone could show him the way.

On the night before he set off, Jamie had stuffed himself with pizza. There was some sort of pizza promotion going on at the hostel. It must also be said that Jamie is not slim. He was probably a stone or so over his ideal weight when he left the hostel. He was and is a strong, healthy young man and chose the best time in his life to put his body through such a punishing ordeal.

What should a human body look like after twelve days with almost no food? In the opinion of many doubters, not like Jamie. Few doctors would make a diagnosis on the basis of TV footage of a young man stepping out of a car, but plenty of people lined up to do just that, including various 'survival experts' and *Sun* doctor, Carol Cooper'. *"He doesn't look like he's lost enough weight. If I didn't know otherwise, I'd guess he'd been camping for the night"*. This was from the *Sun*'s notorious *'Survival of the Fibbest'* article. What the footage also showed was the change in Jamie's facial features, so obvious to anyone familiar with him. The face of the boy posing with the koala bear was round and twinkle eyed. The haunted young man who came back from the dead had eyes opened wide with horror as though watching a train about to run him down. He had gaunt cheek bones, lips and gums receded to expose snaggly teeth. Apart from the weird beard that covered his neck but not his chin, he was scarcely recognisable as the moon faced youth of yore. What the cameras did not show were indications of pneumothoracic emphysema picked up by x-ray or the paralysed thumb and index finger.

Provided water is available, a fit young man ought to be able to last out for about sixty days without food, before delirium, coma and death put an end to the suffering. The Irish republican hunger striker and Mayor of Cork, Terence O'Swiney, succumbed after seventy-four days in Brixton Gaol in 1920. Another well-known republican prisoner, Bobby Sands, survived for sixty-six days during a similar protest in 1981. It may seem crass to say it, but these men starved to death in 'ideal' conditions; conditions that perversely protracted their suffering, accentuated their agony. They were not subjected to extremes of heat, cold or humidity. They were not required to expend precious reserves of energy struggling up and down steep hills, over broken ground, obstructed by undergrowth. Their flesh was not lacerated by thorns or leeches. Nor were they deprived of the company of their fellow men. They knew their relatives knew where they were and why they were refusing food. They received spiritual comfort from priests and prison padres. They were inspired and motivated by a conviction that their sacrifice was a worthy one, in keeping with a historic tradition of Irish resistance.

None of these factors operated in Jamie's case. His chances of surviving without food for anything like as long as these men were nil. There is still a big difference between twelve days and sixty-six, or even seventy-four. Jamie could surely have gone on a few days longer, provided he had access to drinking water. There is plenty of water in this area in winter. Indeed, it provides Sydney with much of its domestic water supply. The watercourses are often deeply incised between steep banks but no fit person should have much difficulty in finding some place where they can get down to the stream. Problems might arise if the water seeker was no longer able to walk or crawl. Jamie did not get to that stage. He had a plastic bottle, so there was no need for him to stay close to the streams or make frequent trips to drink.

Food deprivation can have drastic effects on a person's physical ability to keep moving. It takes about three days for the body to deplete the glucose in the gut and bloodstream, and process available stores of glycerol from the liver. The brain needs about 150 grams of glucose each day. That's equivalent to the weight of about half a standard packet of butter. Once these resources have been used up, the body enters a metabolic condition known as 'starvation mode' when muscle tissue is sacrificed to release 'ketone bodies' in substitute for glucose. Surprisingly, a body in 'starvation mode' tends to preferentially burn up muscle protein, rather than draw on reserves of fat. Mobility may also be compromised by problems in the hips, knees and ankle joints as the tissues that bind the joint together are sacrificed to keep the brain going. There may be pain and internal bleeding at these joints. The lack of essential energy interacts with situational states of mind such as loneliness, guilt, self-pity and anxiety to produce psychological effects - lassitude, irritability, loss of concentration, despair, depression. All of these reactions will impair the victim's potential to make positive, life-saving decisions about what to do to survive. After his initial efforts to find his way out of the labyrinth, Jamie elected to stay put and wait for the choppers to spot him. Sometimes they flew close and he desperately attempted to gain their attention by waving his shirt. With hindsight, it easy to see that he would have been better off trying to find his way out by himself, as indeed he did when he thought the helicopters had given up on him. It was not an easy decision to make, to plunge back into the forest, rather than remain on an outcrop where he believed he was more visible from above. It was vital to resist the urge to give up in despair and let nature take its course. Even the loss of personal cleanliness and sensitivity to one's own body odour can promote despair in someone accustomed to modern standards of hygiene.

There is one other effect of starvation, which would have been known to those who were daily advising on Jamie's ability to survive in the bush. Among the various ways in which the body copes with cold are metabolism of the liver's store of glycerol and the shivering reflex, which works to create heat in the muscles. Once these options are no longer available, an emaciated person's ability to endure low temperatures is drastically reduced. Sensitivity to cold increases. The ability to survive a night in the cold plummets. I never lost the opportunity to assure police, reporters and anyone else that Jamie could tolerate the cold and I am sure that he coped better than most young men in similar night temperatures. I am equally certain that medical experts attached to the search team would have advised that no-one, not even Jamie, could go without food for more than a fortnight without succumbing to exposure in the prevailing conditions. Jamie's achievement was not that he survived twelve days without significant food. That was the easy bit. It was that he was able to survive cold nights with depleted reserves and that he was able to will himself to keep walking, mostly uphill, for mile after mile while depressed, exhausted and aching limbed.

The medical staff who attended Jamie at the Blue Mountain ANZAC Memorial Hospital had no doubt that he had been through twelve days of want and were happy to say so before the rolling cameras of Channel Nine. Yet there are still plenty of folk with giddy confidence in their own wit to offer a second opinion on the basis of what they saw on the telly.

It can also be stated that the New South Wales Police also expressed confidence in the truth of Jamie's story. They spent about two hours debriefing him and were able to form a good understanding of where he had been while they were looking for him. They were able to understand why he had been so difficult to find. The search had concentrated on the route he had taken between Katoomba and Mount Solitary. This was based on solid information about his stated intentions. His last known human contact had taken place at Ruined Castle. He told the couple he met there that he intended to carry on to Mount Solitary. They remembered his Prada t-shirt.

What happened was that he had reached Mount Solitary and then became confused as the path broke up among the rocks on the way down. He followed a false path, probably an animal track, which sent him off down slope in a southerly direction until he was eight or nine miles from the focus of the search. He was also stuck on the far side of Mount Solitary from the point of view of the rescue base located on Kings Tableland so most helicopter flights did not go near him as they shuttled back and forth between Mount Solitary and the helipad. Cedar Creek is off the beaten track. It is heavy going but offers little recompense for that effort in the form of spectacular scenery. Why would any hiker struggle up and down numerous hills, between deeply incised creek valleys, with so little in the way of a decent view to make it worth the while? Even the place names warn you to keep your distance; Growler Ridge, Snarling Dog Creek, Grizzled Dog Ridge. The track that finally led Jamie to his saviours' tent is not a recreational path for bushwalkers. It is there to provide a fire break and an access route for workers who maintain the power line. If Jamie had crossed that track and followed the creeks downstream he would have been even less likely to meet anyone. The various streams join up to form a substantial river or, rather, an elongated lake with steep banks formed by damming the river several miles downstream. It is difficult to follow this river on foot as there are numerous tributary streams too broad to cross without swimming. The area is designated as water catchment for the towns of the Sydney Basin and, as such, is officially out of bounds to walkers.

It is pertinent to ask the sceptics how this kid, fresh to the Blue Mountains, would know enough about the local geography to guess the best place to avoid the searchers, if that had been his perverse intent. On his return, he would need uncanny insight into how the rescue service had conducted their search to be able to say "This is where I was while you were looking for me," and for the police to find it credible.

Chapter Seventeen

The Consolations of Philosophy

Sometime before he left for Australia, in fact while he was still a student at school, Jamie had attempted to trip me up with what probably sounds an odd sort of question for a teenager to ask his old man. For me, the question only became significant in the context of what developed in the aftermath of Jamie's return. Both of us were immaturely inclined to show off 'quite interesting' gobbets of otherwise useless learning, particularly when there are points to be gained from exposing the ignorance of the other side.

"Do you know who is to be found in Dante's inner circle of the betrayers?"

I am by no means intimately familiar with Dante's *'Inferno'* and its concentric circles of hell, though I was not going to tell that to Jamie. I was prepared to make a stab at answering Jamie's challenge for the sake of preserving my reputation as the man who knows most things that are never going to repay the trouble of remembering. "Judas!"

"Yeah".

Now I was struggling.

"Pat Garrett maybe?"

"Who?"

Point to me.

"He's the guy who shot Billy the Kid. Shot The Kid in the arse while he was shafting some senorita. They used to be mates. Before Pat got to be sheriff". As Dylan sang and I wailed, *"Billy, don' it make yah feel so low-down"* pause... *"to be hunted by the man who was your friend?"* Yeah!

"No".

Following on from a charade of rapid stabbing movements, I was eventually able to add the name of Marcus Brutus to the list.

"One to go".

The third and greatest of Dante Alighieri's great betrayers - Lucifer - eluded me.

In recalling this rather bizarre episode of inter-generational mental sparring, it is not my design to set Jamie on pedestal or par with Judas, Lucifer or even Pat Garrett. It is the Brutus connection that invites the following digression and it is Richard who must stand compare. This is not the Brutus who conspired to murder Julius Caesar, but his remote ancestor, Lucius Junius Brutus, who lived four centuries earlier.

In order to persuade Marcus Brutus that he should join a conspiracy to carve up Caesar on the ides of March, Cassius reminded Brutus that one of his illustrious forebears, the first in fact to bear the family name, had taken a leading role in the overthrow of the last king of Rome, Tarquinius Superbus. The very name of Brutus - literally 'brutish' - supposedly recalled this hero's adoption of feigned madness, by which he had diverted attention from a plot to overthrow the king and set Rome up as a republic. In the view urged by Cassius, Julius Caesar aspired to re-establish the institutions of monarchy, with himself as a revived 'King of Rome'. If Caesar should succeed, he would thereby destroy the sacred republic that had emerged from the heroism of the ancestral Brutus.

It therefore became the sad duty of Marcus Brutus to join with Cassius and those other honourable men. They must carve up the upstart Caesar and thereby vouchsafe the institutions of the Roman Republic for future generations. It is never easy to betray a friend, but Brutus had a duty to honour that heroic ancestor and he owed an even higher one to the Senate and People of Rome.

Lucius Brutus himself, the original tyrannicide, had also endured that same searing conflict between duty and affection.

When Caesar succumbed to the flashing blades of his enemies, it was the part played by his beloved Brutus that most deeply cut his heart and framed the last words he ever spoke. It was even rumoured that Brutus was actually Caesar's own extra-marital son. Brutus chose the path of rectitude over that of friendship. He did not live long enough to see the ill consequences of his choice. Nor did the Roman Republic long survive the ministrations of its self-appointed saviours. Brutus's noble sentiments served only to usher in the cruelty and excess of Empire.

There is a fine painting of the older Brutus in the Paris Louvre. The artist is Jacques-Louis David and its catchy title is *'The Lictors Bring to Brutus the Bodies of his Sons'*. The theme is the kind of thing that appealed to the revolutionary spirit of its day - a man who sternly places his duty to the French Republic before ties of paternal affection. Brutus is portrayed sitting awkwardly at home while the bodies of his freshly executed sons are paraded through the house behind him. While the dead youths' momma, sister and slave-girl weep, poppa sits poker faced, staring intently away from the grim procession. On casual inspection he appears to rest his head upon a raised hand, but the hand is actually suspended, claw-like, in mid-air as though Brutus is poised to gouge the eyes from his own face, for it was Lucius Brutus himself who had sat as judge and condemned his own wayward sons to death. The young mens' crime was to conspire with the ousted tyrant king to overthrow the fledgling Roman Republic. As a true stoic, Lucius Brutus does not weep. Emotion is a weakness. He has done his duty. Consequences, whether for good or ill, are of no consequence. It is only those red sandaled feet which betray the inner torment of father Brutus, writhing like fish in a net, tense, contorted, at war one with the other.

Brutus sits in a circle of hell, the circle of righteous fathers who betray their own sons.

As well as my son, I had betrayed the public, the whole damned universe in fact. Pictures of my son and me had been front page news not just in Britain and Australia, but all over the world. We were pictured in papers in Turkey and India and South America. For a few earth days, bug-eyed radio astronomers on a planet that maybe orbits big red Betelgeuse rejoice at glad tidings of my son's comeback from the dead. By the time they pick up the TV signal, we've all been worms' meat for about six centuries. Digitalised images of my gap-toothed grin beam on to the end of time, to the end of the universe. Only that gallant advertiser, the freely delivered and ironically entitled *'My Watford News'*, refused to print my good news. Aloof from all that celebratory frenzy, they elected instead to regale my neighbours with a burnt out car, a drugs raid and some bloke caught masturbating through his lady neighbour's letterbox.

Jamie had survived twelve days adrift in the Eucalyptine Sea, to be greeted on his rescue by the joyful caress of a dad who'd flown half way round the world to find him. The old man had heard the unbelievable news as he sat, crestfallen, about to board the long flight back to London.

But then I had betrayed the boy to the *'Mail on Sunday'*. Maybe the story really was too good to be true after all.

No, I say. It was true. It was the next bit where it all went wrong. When the castle crumbled to ruin. When Mordred strove with Arthur. When strife broke upon Camelot.

Of course there were plenty of people who said it was too good to be true because, as a matter of fact, it wasn't true. When the two of us were sucked into some lesser curlicue of the circle of betrayers, the doubters congratulated themselves on their perspicuity and boasted "We told you so". I sometimes wonder what they would have said if I had actually been the one who found my long lost son. Would anyone have believed that all too perfect ending?

The feel-good story was true. For me, if not for many others, our falling out belonged in another story. It was a sequel, a follow on, not a negation of the tale that went before. For most folk, it was a betrayal. Not of a father by his son, nor of a son by the father, but of humanity as a whole; confirmation, after all, that folk are fundamentally nasty and that money can corrode even the dancing heart of a father blessed by the return of his prodigal son. In a year that featured the crash of banks and all the horrors of war in Iraq and Afghanistan and poor bruised and beaten Baby P., the story of Jamie Neale's remarkable return was one of those too few snippets of perfect news to fill the daily papers. In death, even Michael Jackson was eclipsed. Then I had to come along and spoilt it all by saying something stoopid like "Hey, where's my cut of all that cash on the table?"

That I was motivated by a species of Lucius Brutus rectitude - do the right thing and damn the consequences - was lost on a public that no longer recognised the stern call of duty as taking precedence over ties of dime-store emotion. Jamie had placed me in a position that seemed to me to call into question my integrity and honour. No one cared about that. What mattered was that I had exposed the slime that lay beneath the stone. The beautiful glimmering bubble had burst and, so far as the public was concerned, money was what it was all about. I had learnt my *'Pardoner's Tale'* well, but there were still plenty of people anxious to remind me of this old saw *'Radix mallorum cupiditas est'*. Love of money is the root of evil. In vain might I protest that I hadn't even wanted the money for myself. I was doing it for the searchers,… doing it because what my son had done to me was wrong, very wrong,… doing it because maybe he didn't much care for his dad, despite everything I'd done,… doing it for the sake of two upside down commas in a text message.

I have not set this all down to excuse my role in the ruination of the tale of Jamie's survival. This is not a long-winded apology or an explanation or a suicide note - figuratively speaking. I struggle to explain why things turned out the way they did and not the way things were meant to be. I can only set down what I call the truth, from the privileged position of being aware of some of the thoughts and feelings that caused me to act as I did. Truth is important. The survival of my son, like the nineteenth century survival of Clara Crosbie down in Victoria, has entered the local history of the place where he was lost and found. I have responsibility as a 'primary source' to render a fairly accurate account of my part in those events, lest falsehood become history. If I am biased, it is an honest bias. I do not consciously seek to mislead and, unlike my detractors, I have evidence to back my assertions - an e-mail to Sean that suggesting that fifteen percent was fair recompense for my contribution to the docco. I would have accepted a great deal less, but not 950 dollars less than nothing. That was anything but fair. There are other e-mails that emphasise that I needed the money to make good my promises to donate.

My notions of what other people felt or intended may be inaccurate, but I can personally testify to the effect of these notions, accurate or otherwise, on my own feelings and behaviour. If, in seeking to tell the truth, I set down confusion, or inaccuracy or inconsistency then that is because some things seemed confused or fuzzy or contradictory at the time and may continue to do so to me today. I cannot set down anyone else's motives or reasons. There may be actions, on my part, which seem ill-matched by what purports to be their motivation, and I dare say my detractors will say that no man can be best placed to examine his own motivation. I may be lying to the public or else unaware of my own true motivation. Speculative explanations of my petulant behaviour include jealousy of my son's sudden acquisition of riches, so much in contrast to his father's years of toil with very little to show for it, irritation that the media spotlight had swung decisively away from me to focus squarely on my son. In each scenario, it is assumed that I was myself unaware of the malefic incubus gnawing at my psyche.

I was actually very happy for my son to make enough money to be financially independent three years earlier than I had anticipated. I was certainly unhappy that he should have done so by selling, not just his own story of dauntless survival, but also my own story of emotional ups and downs in searching for him. To me, if not to others, it seemed shabby and ungracious in the particular circumstances of our joyful reunion. I was not looking to gain wealth for myself through his ordeal.

As for the charge of 'hogging the limelight' and therefore being unable to cope when media attention shifted from 'talked out' dad to 'untold son', I believe my record in the face of media blandishments is in stark contrast to this picture. I gave interviews at the hospital only when asked to do so by the hospital management. Their intention was to relieve media pressure on the hospital by offering footage for the reporters to pack up and go away with. I did it for free and I did it willingly, I may even have enjoyed it, but I would not have done it if the hospital hadn't okayed and encouraged it. On my return to the UK, I gave one, very reluctant interview to the *'Mail on Sunday'*, following on from my failed brinkmanship, and an interview on Radio-5-live to counter the canard that I had demanded half my son's money. I was also dismayed that most people seemed unable to understand or accept that I did not want the Channel Nine money for myself and I sought to clarify that I had broken no 'agreement' to accept money for my flights and bar tab nor was I accusing Jamie of breaching any agreement to 'split the money in half', as widely attributed to me. I was offered many other opportunities to 'enter the limelight', including a couple passed on by Sean after he ceased to represent me. I turned them all down. I do not deny that I did enjoy blabbing to the cameras when things were going well. Nor was I the only one. There were policemen and medical staff who were also visibly as pleased as Punch to be on the telly. It's a common and harmless condition.

After my story became contentious, all such pleasure evaporated. What I did not understand about this decision to shun further exposure was the way news media rush to fill the vacuum presented by a person's refusal to cooperate. Speculation and made-up stories spring up to replace whatever truths the recluse might have otherwise have to offer, just as one paper's exclusivity creates another paper's licence to publish lies. My withdrawal from the fray did not end the parade of stories about me and my son. Jamie's much-quoted refusal 'to engage in a slanging match with my father' was contrasted with my own indiscretion. Meanwhile, 'sources' and some spokesperson called 'It is believed that' were happy to brief the press about this 'dysfunctional dad' who 'walked out on his son' and who resented the way 'media attention' had shifted away from him. If only I too had had an agent to speak up for me, while I personally maintained a dignified silence. I acknowledge that I was the idiot who ramped up the war and maybe cannot complain when it turned against me.

My main animus was directed against my former agent. This was not the populist tale of two Poms who took Australia for a ride. No one gypped Australia, neither me nor Jamie. It was the tale of one Aussie publicity agent who failed to appreciate he had two clients - two intelligent adults who both expected to be consulted and remunerated for arrangements he made on their behalf. On the Wednesday we signed up to Sean, we could have signed up to any one of about two hundred press organisations clamouring for our approval. Of course Jamie was hotter property than me, but I too had something to offer a switched-on media agent. I had, as Holly Byrnes acidly put it, *'crafted the image of a perfect parent'* and was sincerely committed to making money to pay back to Australia. Anyone but Sean would have appreciated that I could be an asset to their portfolio not some awkward hanger-on to be taken for a mug. Could any man on the planet, let alone someone holding out media expertise, have made a more ham-fisted job of representing our interconnected interests? I had signed up to an agreement and I believed Sean had failed to deliver. In the space of seven days, he transformed me from *'world's coolest dad'* to world's most reviled parent on antipodal continents. This supposed media guru had orchestrated an unnecessary PR disaster out of the most heart-warming story to emerge from New South Wales in a generation.

This has been also been a saga of three English peoples' interaction with the continent of Australia, stretching back to my mum's arrival as a teenage mother back in 1954. Thereby also hangs the tale of a certain tragic flaw which has cascaded down those three generations from mother to son to grandson. This flaw consists in an exaggerated esteem for our respective mental faculties, symptomised by refusal to consent to any arrangements made on our behalf without our being consulted as intelligent adults. I remember being outraged at once being asked whether I suffered from 'vessel disease'. The nurse had clearly taken me for a buffoon who would fail to understand what she meant by 'vascular disease'. Even my lady mother, despite her hearing difficulties would bristle at being expected to consent to anything without consultation. 'I may be deaf, but I ain't daft' would be her politer response to being patronised. Neither mum, nor Jamie, nor I submit to being bullied or blackmailed or taken for a ride. Provided we are treated with consideration, we can, each in his or her own way, be perfectly affable, generous and obliging - just don't take it for granted! Sean seemed, if anything, to have a hysterical aversion to discussing anything with me. He was happy to discuss the Channel Nine deal with Jamie but not with me. He was happy to discuss my *'Sun'* proposal with Jamie but not with me. He was happy to advise Jamie that 'the pretty Irish lass' wished to get in touch with me, but not tell me about it. So much for client confidentiality! Did he think I was so imbecilic I needed my son to be my keeper? I came to reciprocate the contempt which Sean had shown for me, but I would still have been prepared to negotiate with him. Sean abdicated the role of deal broker. He maintained that it was up to me and Jamie to settle our differences - essentially for me to petition Jamie to please let me have my money so I can pass it on to those deserving Aussies. What a complete Arsehole!

When Jamie said "Don't pay my dad. He doesn't want anything", surely Sean had a contractual duty to ask me if that was truly my position? Had he done so and negotiated separate appearance fees, all three of us would today be happier. Jamie had not been impressed with Sean either, though he became less hostile once I had become the primary object of his rancour.

I must therefore bear the responsibility for the ruination not just of my image as a decent, well-meaning parent but also for the breach that estranged my adult children from me. It was the clash of my own constitutional inability to put up with being gypped and Jamie's refusal to be blackmailed into coughing up the proceeds that set us on our collision course. The impasse would have been just as deep if the roles had been reversed, with the important proviso that I would never have been so churlish in the first place.

In the year 2000, primatologists Frans de Waal and Sarah Brosnan conducted a series of experiments to investigate *'Attitudinal Reciprocity in Food Sharing among Brown Capuchins'*. Two monkeys, separated by a wire mesh screen, were encouraged to expend their joint pulling power to drag a weighted tray into the cage to obtain food. Only one of the partnership gained the reward. The second capuchin only got rewarded for their effort if the winner was prepared to share the food through the mesh that separated them. "They seemed to realise when help was needed and rewarded those who provided it" (*'Our Inner Ape'*, Frans de Waal, Granta Books 2005).

In another investigation (*'Payment for Labour in Monkeys'* de Waal and Bergman, *Nature*, 2000), two monkeys were initially rewarded with slices of cucumber for performing a set task. The pair performed happily until one of them was rewarded with grapes instead of cucumber. The hard-done-by partner refused to continue, sometimes hurling the cucumber out of the cage in disgust. By the end of the test, the loser "sat sulking in the corner". The common ancestors of modern man and that malcontented South American monkey ceased to intermingle genes about thirty million years ago. My son is, of course, separated from me by just a single generation. Oh, but oh, my little simian friend, how I second your emotion! If the unfairness I suffered was so obvious that even a brown capuchin monkey gets it, why did the public not understand? Much was to do with Jamie's status as a vulnerable young adult recovering from his traumatic experience. In the eyes of the world, I was not a hard-done-by co-worker, but a sinister Svengalic manipulator, setting out to exploit my son's celebrity. I should be grateful he was alive, not carping about a few thousand quid. When the boy refused to play ball and hand over 'half his money', I had vindictively complained to the media. But I had not been vindictive. I had offered Jamie a choice between behaving badly and doing the decent thing. Bizarrely enough, doing the decent thing would have ultimately enabled him to earn more than the alternative, as well as getting me off the hook of my promise to donate but no money to do it with. It ought to have been a 'no-brainer', but I had miscalculated just how cussed a traumatised teenager can be. I suspect Jamie may also have miscalculated that I would be too embarrassed to follow through with my threat to go public. I wish now, as I wished then, that Jamie had had the sense to make such meaningful concessions as might enable me to withdraw my threat without further loss of face. Instead, he simply threatened not to talk to me ever again if I dared to follow through. Like those tray hauling monkeys, we could have both been winners. I would have vindicated my integrity. Jamie would have money to buy a flat.

I was chronologically the more mature out of Jamie and me and I ought to have exercised more patience and understanding at what was, for both of us, a strange and stressful time. Maybe, if I had not been so post-traumatically crazy myself, I might have been mature enough to let it go, but having already taken three massive kicks in the kisser since Jamie came marching home, I was not in that blessed frame of mind. I was the monkey who didn't even get the cucumber, let alone the grape.

I should have grasped the olive branch Jamie offered me, regardless of my cynicism about its sincerity. Instead, I was sure that Jamie, guided by Sean, would have the wisdom to settle with me. Then we could rebuild our relationship without my feeling resentment at his breach of trust. I allowed hurt feelings to drive my actions. Once I had made commitments to *'The*

Mail on Sunday', my reluctance to break an undertaking made it difficult for me to withdraw from what I had agreed, despite my having realised that I had made a mistake. The other problem was that the *'The Sun'* had become aware of the problems between Jamie and me and were able to run their own, highly inaccurate, parody of the affair - a version which became the definitive account for most of the other reports. Dad wants half the cash, Jamie has only 'agreed' to pay expenses. The cat was out of the bag and I could not put it back.

I admire the Graeco-Roman guide to behaviour broadly classified as Stoicism. It is a philosophy which emphasises honourable dealing, fearless rectitude and calmness in the face of adversity. It also advocates a healthy disdain for the trappings of wealth and power. I had not been calm in the face of Jamie's discourtesy. I should have let it go. Today I am still at something of a loss to explain why I could not do that. What I can say is that it was not the deal done to deprive me of any share of the money that drove me to anger. He was wrong to do it - all the more so in that it left me with nothing to honour my promises. Those promises were important to me, regardless of whether anyone else cared about my keeping them. It felt wretched to be put in a position of not being able to do as I had said I would. But I was able to walk away from the confrontation. I thought there would be other chances to sell my story and fulfil those promises.

Jamie was wrong to disparage my decision to join the search for him before the rolling cameras of Channel Nine. The comments were not broadcast. I did not know that at the time. Even if had known, I would still have found the dismissal hurtful. The story did become public, through Holly Byrnes' ill-informed gutter journalism in the Aussie *'Telegraph'*. *"Cass was believed to be upset by... Sources said ... It is understood ..."* The lack of an attributed source is significant and typical of Holly. She never attempted to check anything with me, despite my having given my e-mail address to her colleague, Tim Verotel. When she cited my words about not profiting from the media, she simply took it as read that these promises must be hollow and insincere. On what evidence? Dad rows with son: *ergo* Dad will break his word to the Australian people. It's what we philosophers are pleased to call a *non sequitur*.

I did not know that Jamie was mad with me because he thought I had put the phone down on his mother. He should have spoken about that, rather than nourished resentment over something that never happened. We both live with the consequences. I did not make a scene. I told him I was unhappy. He whined about me giving him a hard time. The steam was rising.

When I flew back to London, I had no thought of creating problems for my son. It was only after I read his text message that I flipped. I received the text just as I left Bounds Green Underground Station. I was tired and jet lagged after my twenty three hour flight. I had a long walk ahead of me and heavy bags to carry. My elation had evaporated. I had come down from the emotional high that had begun five days before. The text not only vetoed me from any prospect of talking to *'The Sun'* , but also seemed to rule out any other access to the media. Jamie was gagging me. He didn't want me giving interviews because he was embarrassed by my talk of donating money to the relevant agencies. That was how I read it. It was the inverted commas of 'love' Jamie that left me fuming at all this. Why had he taken the trouble to add these punctuation marks? Text messages are axiomatically brief, with severely truncated spellings and punctuation. Inverted commas are used, among other things, to denote irony, to indicate that a word is being used in a manner different from its usual connotation. The text seemed to mock those previous twenty years of hard work to be a decent dad to my children, juggling time and money and Jean to do whatever I needed to do to see they didn't lose out. Like all offspring, self-included, Jamie took it for granted. I had defined myself in terms of my fatherhood of Clair and Jamie. I had curtailed my love-life, lost sleep, changed from one set of clothes to another by the side of the road as I hurried sleepless from one job to another. It should all have been worth it. All given without grudge for the love of my children. When they didn't give a damn, it seemed unfair. If I really had walked out and put their needs behind me, could they have appreciated me any the less?

I once watched a TV documentary about the life of a dung beetle. The film followed the female from the time she emerged from the warm, wet mud of the Sudan, until her moment of passing and beyond. The intervening months were taken up by the gargantuan task of gathering together a great big gobstopper of elephant dung and rolling her burden across the savannah. Then she buried it all in a hole under the ground - literally, digging her own grave. She laid her eggs in the great big dung ball. Just as she finished sealing off the chamber where the eggs would ride out the dry season, she took leave of this vale of tears, this life of endless toil, keeled over onto her back with six spindly legs in the air. A few months later, the rains loosened this rock hard tomb with a womb and a new brood of tiny scarabs came scuttling out from the dung. Heedless of Momma's sacrifice, they streamed on by. Those wispy, lifeless legs shudder as the torrent of baby beetles buffets mum's carcass aside in the headlong scramble to get out and get stuck into some elephant shit. I was strangely moved by it all. I recognised myself in that poor dead dung beetle. I too had trundled my massive burden of crap around the world to try to be a decent dad but it meant as little to my children as it did to those hatchlings. I recognised it was only natural and normal and that one day those newly metamorphosed mini-beasts will endure similar indifference when they make sacrifices for their own hatchlings. But it was still so sad.

Jean Buriden is not well known, even among academic philosophers. If he is known at all, it is his donkey that takes centre stage as 'Buriden's Ass'. This does the fourteenth century Picard a disservice. His contribution to the rise of scientific rationalism was significant and, as for the ass, Buriden neither owned the beast nor wrote about it. Buriden challenged the ancient orthodoxy that an inanimate object can move only while it is continually subject to an outside force. He recognised that Aristotle's attempt to explain why a thrown stone continues to fly through the air, even after it has left the 'force' of the thrower's hand, was unsustainable. He realised that a moving body does not come to rest because it is no longer being forced to move, but because something progressively impedes its progress. He coined the term 'impetus' to explain why a thrown stone does not drop directly to earth when the thrower's hand ceases to apply a push. This was advanced thinking for its time. Aristotle was regarded as more or less infallible in the fourteenth century and it was an age when the truth of these matters was settled by appeal to established authority rather than by observation or experiment. Buriden's insight tipped the domino that tumbled down a line through Copernicus and Galileo to Isaac Newton and beyond. The modern world owes this man a drink, not a donkey.

Buriden's description of the physical universe as a mechanistic system in which everything happens because something caused it to happen is close to modern scientific thinking, excluding such delights as quantum mechanics. Things happen, not so much because it pleases God for them to happen, but because they could not have happened otherwise, given the conditions that preceded them. This is scientific determinism. It is applicable to the world of solid objects in relation to the passage of time Much more controversial is the role of determinism in human behaviour. The debate polarises round the role of 'free will', whether people are able to choose aspects of their destiny or whether the 'choices' we make are determined by the information available to us at the time, interacting with fundamental urges to act in our own interest or in satisfaction of biological drives. From a religious perspective, free will is important. Without human free will, God appears to be punishing sinners for decisions that were determined at the beginning of time, choices they had no choice but to make. Buriden's opponents recognised that determinism undermines the grace of God and they conceived the thought experiment of 'Buriden's Ass' to caricature his teaching. The ass is centrally positioned between two equally luscious bundles of hay. According to this travesty of Buriden's thinking, the ass has no overriding reason to choose to eat from one bundle over the other. According to cod-Buriden determinism, the donkey eternally hesitates to make a choice, pending clarification that never comes. The beast starves to death.

Alternatively and as would certainly happen in any effort to replicate the given scenario, the donkey appreciates that the choice lies not between right hoof and left hoof hay but between sustenance and starvation and goes on to choose either. Yet my son spent twelve days on a rock in Australia pondering which way to go, or stay. He might have starved or frozen to death within ten miles of Katoomba town. Thankfully he made a choice and walked. It took the withdrawal of the choppers to stimulate that life-saving decision. So maybe Buriden's Ass does need some kind of nudge to make its choice.

The experiment would be even more interesting if some outcome of very real consequence hung upon the donkey's choice. Let us suppose that the life of Buriden's as yet unmarried father depends on whether the donkey chooses left or right, that the King of France has decided to judge a difficult case by reference to the donkey's behaviour - right bundle leads on to birth of Buriden and the modern world, left bundle, the prisoner hangs and the world lingers on in medieval scholasticism. It would be a defeat for determinism whichever way the donkey turned. If the right bundle is favoured, the determinist philosopher emerges by the ass's exercise of free will. If the donkey turns left - no Buriden. Of course determinism wins if the donkey starves to death and Jean Buriden's dad, rather like Schrodinger's cat, remains eternally in suspense of suspension.

There are elements of determinism in the system known as Stoicism, but a stoic donkey would realise that it did have control over its own thinking, would eat and live. Stoicism is not a religion but a set of sentiments designed to avoid a life of futile despair. The goal of stoicism is not salvation in the next world nor happiness in this one, but 'ataraxia' - a state of unruffled acceptance of all the world can throw at a man. In the second century AD, the leading Stoic philosophers were Epictetus, a manumitted slave, and the Emperor - Marcus Aurelius. Epictetus taught that there are things which we have exclusive power over, such as our judgment, desires, attitudes etc. Then there are things we either cannot control or may not be able to control, such as the state of our health, or the activities of others. The system reconciles determinism with free will. Epictetus's most frequently quoted statement of this asserts "I am put in chains. Must I then lament? I must go into exile. Does any man hinder me from going with smiles and cheerfulness and contentment?"

It is, of course, possible to dispute about how much control we can exert over our feelings and judgments, particularly at a time of extreme adversity. Epictetus seems to have believed it was essentially a matter of understanding the 'true nature of things', that nothing is good or bad in itself but only thinking makes it so, as parodied in the speech by Hamlet. The task is to control the thinking - which is supposedly within our control. The 'true nature of things' refers to the inescapable order of the universe. Marcus Aurelius seems to concur with this. The *'Meditations'* of Marcus Aurelius are thought to have been assembled for the emperor's private contemplation rather than for publication or with a view to influencing others. As such, much of the material is trite or derivative or what might otherwise be regarded as plagiaristic. This is verse 9, translated from the Greek by Gregory Hays;

'Whatever happens to you has been waiting to happen since the beginning of time. The strands of fate wove both of them together,... your own existence and the things that happen to you'.

I alluded to this long view of the workings of fate when I began this book. I suggested that my son would not have got lost if it had not been for certain sands, washed down from the super-continent of Pangaea, to settle in a warm Triassic sea. Those sediments ultimately created the geology that gave rise to the scenery that drew my son to Mount Solitary. Determinism in action.

So, how does this surfeit of philosophy, both classical and medieval, bear upon my decision to choose a future of estrangement from the son I love? It has to be said that most folk do not need to be told by an obscure second-century philosopher that it is not a good idea to act under the influence of a passion. Or that, while I cannot influence the build-up of sand in ancient seas, I can decide not to go through with threats after my ultimatum is rejected. I should be sufficiently gratified that Jamie still exists to endure the slings and arrows of my son's post-traumatic insolence 'with smiles and cheerfulness and contentment'. Both Jean (Neale, not Buriden) and brother Jeff could work that out and I suspect that most people would not have made the decision I made. In the modern world, feelings are more highly valued than was the case in the Classic Era, but feelings of outrage and hurt should not overcome feelings of paternal tenderness or self-interest. Duty not to allow a promise to go unfulfilled was also part of the brew, but while that may have scored highly with Aurelius and Epictetus, such sanctimoniousness is regarded today more as a vice than a virtue. There can be no doubt I should have acted otherwise, indeed could have acted otherwise. Unfortunately, despite having an advisor at his side who had pretensions to be a skilled negotiator, the other side were not prepared to concede anything that might ease the humiliation of my withdrawal from the dispute, nor did I relish a future relationship with a son gloating about his having swindled me and then having faced me down when I insisted on redress. I didn't act otherwise and the unchangeable past is a feature of the cosmic order, the things over which we have no control. Since I cannot hope to be happy in a situation where I, quondam *'World's Coolest Dad'*, no longer have meaningful contact with my son and daughter, I must strive to achieve something close to that state of serene acceptance of what I cannot change, identified as 'ataraxia' by the stoics of Ancient Rome.

For me, the biggest surprise in the fallout from those two weeks in July is the manner in which my relationship with Jean has strengthened. I assumed that, like Clair, she would shun me for what I had done to our family. When the children were young, I had looked forward to the day when they were old enough to decide for themselves how much they wished to see of their father. I obtained my court order and became just another sad, Sunday afternoon dad, traipsing my beloved children round museums and zoos and ancient ruins. I worked two jobs to get the money to buy a house where, one day, we could all live together, free from Jean That day never came. Now they are grown up and I see nothing of Clair and Jamie, but I do go out with Jean. We go round museums and ruins together and return to the house I bought for our children; drink tea together on the patio my son helped to build. The future seldom pans out the way you expect.

I know Epictetus would disapprove, but I do dream of the way I wanted it to be. When I find my son and we sit down in a pub in Katoomba together, Jeff, Jamie and me. We enjoy a pint and a pie restore to Jamie to his old strength and self and I go over the things I had wanted to say to him in the days when I'd thought he was dead. There are no reporters or agents or offers of money about, just the people we met on the trail, the wonderful guys and gals who searched for him and shared in my ecstasy when he came through okay. We party through the night and, in the sunshine of another day, the three of us sit in the front of the van with Jamie in the middle for the drive back to Botany Bay and our flight back to Blighty and, as the van turns east along that Great Western Highway, the train chuffing along the track beside us lets rip with its whistle and a kangaroo starts up from the bush and bounds along the road ahead, fat tail a-swish across its backside, while Jeff quips, "There goes Skippy. Where the hell was he when all this stuff was going on?"

And we all laugh together in unison like at the end of a Scooby Doo cartoon. That would have been great.

Appendices

i) My contract with Sean.

ii) Just a couple of the e-mails that flashed back and forth as I tried to get Sean and Jamie to address my grievance. I am ashamed of the belligerent tone but they do make it clear that I was not asking for 'half Jamie's money' and also that I was distressed at not being able to make the promised donations. I reckoned fifteen per cent of the payment would have been fair to me, but I would have taken less, even a good deal less, if it had been offered. To me, this was not 'Jamie's money' but appearance money for my contribution to the documentary. The reference to 'not now' sounds bad, but was a negotiating device. I was hoping we could settle for fifteen per cent, rather than some lesser offer from their side.

iii) Three newspaper reports charting my apotheosis, apodiabolosis and partial rehabilitation at the hands of the press. All three contain significant factual errors. I have paid out about seven hundred pounds for the right to reprint the respective intellectual property of Holly Byrnes and Dave Murray. Coming on top of the thousand dollars I laid out for Nick Greenaway's bar bill, I seem to be standing drinks for half the media folk in Australia! In Holly's case, this is all the more galling in that the implication of her report is that I was not entitled to be paid for the intellectual property I disseminated on Channel Nine. Stuart Jeffries and *'The Guardian'* were gracious enough to waive their royalty fee.

iv) My tribute to my lost son as delivered to the search parties on Saturday 11th July 2009.

I refer to our meeting on 16th July 2009 and our agreement is as follows;

1. You appoint me as your agent for a period of 12 months commencing on the date of this letter.
2. My appointment as your agent is exclusive and worldwide.
3. I will handle all commercial opportunities in relation to the use of your name, image, likeness and story during the term of this agreement.
4. My commission from all activities set out in paragraph 3 shall be: (a) 17.5% on all income received.
5. All income referred to in paragraph 4 above shall be paid to my company first and shall be remitted to you after deduction of my commission. All income must be remitted to you within 7 days of receipt by me.
6. Either party shall have the right to terminate this agreement by notice in writing in the event that other party is in breach of this agreement which is incapable of remedy, or, if capable of remedy, is not remedied within 7 days following service of written notice of such breach.
7. All agreements entered into must be signed by you. I do not have the authority to bind you or sign agreements on your behalf. For the avoidance of doubt, it is agreed that you will have total control over any arrangement you enter into and the final say on all offers and contracts and that I will not agree to any arrangement nor commit you without consulting with you first and obtaining your instructions regarding any such arrangement.
8. I will use my best endeavours to maximise all commercial opportunities presented, negotiate contracts as your agent and bring to your attention all offers and contracts regarding your story.

9. The terms of this agreement shall remain strictly private and confidential. Such confidentially *(sic)* shall continue both during and following the conclusion of the term of this agreement.

It would be appreciated if you would confirm your acceptance of the terms of this agreement by signing and dating below.

Best regards, Sean Anderson,
Managing Director

Monday July 20th 2009
Subject: termination of contract

Dear Sean, I am invoking clause 6 of our contract dated 16th July. I feel that you are in breach of clause 8, whereby you undertake to 'use your best endeavours' to maximise all commercial opportunities presented. you set me up a deal with Chanel 9 *(sic)* and all I got was a bar-tab, a bed a car ride and a chopper in exchange for interview, stills pictures and farewell footage. According to Jamie, you supported him in denying me a chance to talk to the Sun from the 'that's my boy you're calling a liar' angle. I don't need an agent who sells his client's story for nothing and places barriers to other outlets. As I said in my last e-mail, I was surprised that you had nothing lined up for me in the UK. By denying me opportunities to make money, you have placed me in a difficult position with regard to agencies who have been promised money from anything I get. by the terms of our contract, you have seven days to remedy the breach I have outlined. i hope you will accept the breach as final. i will be carrying on on the assumption that you will be doing nothing and that the breach will not be remedied. Could you please acknowledge receipt of this e-mail. regards from Richard Cass

Hi Richard,

I'm in the final stages of organising a deal for Jamie for a documentary on his experience.

They will want to interview you as well in London - should take an hour or so. I have negotiated a *(sic)* interview fee of 1,000 pounds for you. Is this ok with you?

Sean

Managing Director

22 Management : Representing the Best

Wednesday July 22nd 2009

subject: Re. let's sort this out

Sorry Sean, you're too late. you know I want out and I believe you're stringing me along. I note that our agreement commits you to "not agree to any arrangement nor commit you (ie. Richard Cass) without consulting your instructions regarding any such arrangement". This did not take place prior to the channel nine deal and, if it had, take it as read that I would not have agreed to sell my story for a burger and a bar-tab.

This is clearly a 'breach that is incapable of remedy'. So I regard myself as no longer your client. I am in contact with uk media - so much for your 'resistance is futile' crap - I don't want to spoil my son's party, but he, you and channel nine will not be smelling of roses if I go public. I am open to negotiation - a substantial percentage of the Channel nine pot and a definite release form *(sic)* my contract with you should do the trick. Sean, it did not have to be this way. I would have been happy with 15% of the channel9 money (not now though!). Jamie should not have slagged me off on tv. You should have let me run with the sun rebuttal. The 24 hour embargo was about to lapse so there was no problem there - just more crap. Jamie's gratuitously insulting text was the final straw. I believe you have been gagging me because my message about paying my money back to the good causes was embarrassing for Jamie. I have no problem with what Jamie does with what he gets. He is a young kid about to go to university, he needs it. I would make it clear that my promises are personal to me. Jamie's nineteen and he will make his own arrangements. he says he does recognise his obligations and will be making donations, which is fine by me. In other words we could and should have kept this a feelgood story. if we can get out of this without pissing in my son's porridge, I would be happy to take part in this documentary and happy for you to take your cut what's on offer for it, but I now need my own agent and I feel there is a conflict of interest when you are representing both of us. I do so wish we had phoned both names on the list, rather than tossed a coin and got you. regards from Richard.

Is Richard Cass the world's coolest dad?

by Stuart Jeffries, *The Guardian (UK)* 16th July 2009.

Picture the scene. Your teenage son has been missing for 12 days in the densely wooded Blue Mountains of New South Wales. You've given up hope that he'll ever be found and you've buried a red rose in the outback in a 'closure ceremony'. And then, just as you're boarding the plane back to London, you get a text saying he's been found alive and well.

Few fathers in such circumstances would have managed as jaunty press conference speech as the one Richard Cass pulled off yesterday. I would have been more of a blubbing, incoherent wreck that usual.

"I can't say I'll kill him because that would spoil the point of him coming back," joked Cass, "but yeah I'm going to kick his arse because of the millions that have been spent on the search, the man hours and woman hours that have gone into it". Press conferences aren't supposed to be like this. Nobody goes off script, and it is axiomatic that no one ever sounds even vaguely human.

Cass broke those rules. He said his 19-year-old son Jamie was "a stupid kid" who'd put a lot of Australians to a lot of trouble. As his exasperated Dad pointed out, he was the only teenager in the world who goes on a 10 mile hike and leaves his mobile phone behind. His plans prior to this were to go to south-east Asia, but he can forget that now. He's put his mother through enough.

In a world where politicians are media trained into systematic speciousness, where relatives respond only with clichés when asked to comment on the greatest dramas in their children's lives, Cass was a joy to hear. Even his praise for the rescuers was sweetly graceful. During the Ashes, to hear an Englishman salute the Australians was the most unlikely thing of all.

Copyright: Guardian News and Media. All rights reserved.

Richard Cass flies home to sell story "Asked for half of 60 Minutes money" Jamie Neale's agent confirms "rift"

by Holly Byrnes, *Daily Telegraph* (Sydney) July 25th 2009

HE WAS lost in the wilderness, cold and hungry for 12 days.

Now Jamie Neale has been abandoned by his father, who has rushed home to London to be the first to sell his son's amazing tale of survival to the British press.

Less than 24 hours after the 19-year-old was released from hospital still suffering the effects of hypothermia and exhaustion, his father Richard Cass left his son behind in Sydney in a dash home to cash in on the backpacker's misadventure.

Cass, who told Australian media last week he was not interested in profiting from his son's rescue and survival story, is understood to have asked his son for a 50 per cent share of Neale's deal with Channel 9's *60 Minutes* program.

Not content with his son's offer to cover his father's airfares and the cost of a drinks celebration with rescue workers at Hotel Gearin in Katoomba, Cass was also believed to be upset by his son's treatment of him during the Tara brown interview.

Neale hinted at the pair's estranged relationship when he told *60 Minutes* he was "surprised" his father had flown to Sydney to join the rescue effort.

The admission is understood to have angered Cass, who had crafted a perfect parent image with the media.

Neale had refused his father's plea to split the $100,000 he was paid for his story, while honouring his pledge to donate proceeds from the deal to the emergency services who helped find him.

Cass admitted he had given up hope of finding his son and was booked on a flight back to London before rescuers called off their search on Wednesday last week.

Neale had been unable to fly home on medical grounds, seeking specialist treatment for damage to his lungs after being exposed to the elements during his bush ordeal.

He is believed to be staying in Bondi while awaiting the green light from his doctors.

Neale's Australian agent Sean Anderson confirmed the "rift" yesterday and reports that Cass had sold his story to London's *Sunday Mirror*.

"I can confirm there is a rift between him and his father," he said.

"I am not in a position to go into details of that falling out. Richard emailed me to tell me he has done a deal with a newspaper in the UK but ultimately that is a matter for Jamie and his father to resolve".

Sources said Cass and Neale had long had a "dysfunctional" relationship after the father walked out on his family when his son was three.

The falling out is understood to have coincided with the media's attention shifting from father to son, with Nine insiders revealing that Cass had written to *60 Minutes* claiming he had been overlooked for a hamburger order, when the crew stopped for lunch last Friday.

Neale's mother Jean blasted her ex-husband for seeking payment, telling *The Sun* newspaper: "His behaviour is outrageous".

"He phoned me yesterday to say he was selling his story because he was angry Jamie is refusing to share the money with him," she said.

Copyright: News Limited

Richard Cass regrets falling out with backpacker son Jamie Neale over money. by David Murray. *Daily Telegraph* (Sydney) October 16th 2009.

The father of British backpacker Jamie Neale who survived 12 days lost in the Blue Mountains, is desperate to reconcile with his son after a bitter falling-out over money.

Richard Cass yesterday revealed his regrets at becoming estranged from Jamie after an argument over payment for a *60 Minutes* interview about the ordeal.

On returning to the UK, Mr Cass complained to a newspaper that his 19 year old son had not split the money with him as previously agreed. "I love my son. that interview was a mistake" Mr Cass said outside his modest home in Watford, northwest of London. "It also got me misunderstood. There were guys saying 'Who is this money-grubbing bastard?' which is not me".

He wanted the money not for himself but to pass on to the rescuers.

"If I'd got the money I would have given it away as that's what I said I would do. It's difficult to convey to people that you can be annoyed at not getting money when you've announced your intention to give it away," he said. "It's like if you said to your boss, 'I'm going to give my pay to Children in Need at the end of the week' and he said 'Well, you don't want the money. I'm not going to pay you'."

Mr Cass revealed he had donated his fee of almost $10,000 from his interview with the UK's *Daily Mail (sic)* to the Blue Mountains Hospital. "I said outside the hospital that I was not going to make any money out of it and I didn't," he said.

A special-needs teacher, Mr Cass lives in a working class neighbourhood and drives a small, old model car.

"I feel that I've done as much as I can for the rescuers," he said. "I've given the money away that I got. I fell out with my son because I couldn't give the money that I promised. And if I get any more money I will give it to them".

Setting the record straight about deals done in the wake of the rescue, Mr Cass said his son had not received $200,000 as widely reported.

Instead his son was given $100,000 and a pledge from Channel 9 to provide $100,000 in advertising to inform the community about safe hiking.

"He pays his commission and then has various expenses. Out of the remainder he did give a donation to the SES and the hospital and also to the people who found him, though I don't know if they accepted it." Mr Cass said.

Jamie last month said he donated a total of $16,000 to the various agencies that helped him.

The backpacker, who is back living in London, yesterday directed calls to his Australian agent.

Copyright: News Ltd

A father's tribute to his lost boy

Last night I was unable to sleep, so I have tried to put together some words to convey something of what my family has lost if my son remains unfound.

Every father will say that his own sons and daughters are special. But I will set down some of the facts and aspirations of my son's life so far that defy anyone to say that this boy was common clay.

There is much concern in my country about the behaviour of young men – with blame for their perceived shortcomings to be blamed on family breakdown. Jamie came from a 'broken home'. I forgot to marry his mother and we ceased to live together when he was three years old. He was raised by his single mother on a council estate in North London. But this was a teenager who was never in trouble with the police, who left school last summer with A-levels in Maths, Chemistry and History. He worked through winter and spring as a lab technician to raise cash for his trip and intended to go to Exeter University as soon as he returned. He was a blood donor and a duke of Edinburgh Award recipient. He was kind and courteous to everyone. But this was no humourless paragon of virtue. Jamie was intrigued to learn that Karl Marx was buried just up the road from where he lived, so the two of us popped up to Highgate to call on him – not through any left wing leanings, just to get in touch with history. I thought no more of it, but when Jamie stepped out to see the world in June 2009, he was intending to fly on from Australia to Hanoi and Moscow. I was astonished to hear that he wanted to call on Lenin and ho Chi Minh. I believe any teenager who can arrange his tour of the world around the brilliant conceit of tracking down the cadavers of Communist dictators is very, very special indeed.

I also wish to say that I am extremely grateful to the NSW police, Park Rangers and others who have contributed so much time and effort in the search for Jamie Neale. I know that they will continue to strive to find him as long as any flicker of hope remains that he may still survive. When I fly back to London, I know that this land has done all it could do to send him home to his mother and, for that, I thank the people of Australia from the bottom of my heart.

Made in the USA
Charleston, SC
08 November 2012